AF405433

Effective
Questioning
& Listening
Skills

Gerard Assey

Effective
Questioning & Listening Skills

By
Gerard Assey

© Copyright 2024 by Author

Published by:
Gerard Assey
19/18, Palli Arasan Street
Anna Nagar East
Chennai - 600 102

ISBN: 978-81-967202-0-9

All Rights Reserved. No part of this publication may be reproduced, stored in a retrieval system, or transmitted in any form or by any means- electronic or mechanical, including photocopying, recording, or by any information storage and retrieval system, without prior written permission from the author.

(Image courtesy starline on freepik: www.Freepik.com-Thank You)

Table of Contents

- Preface
- Understanding the Audience
- The Purposes of Questioning
- Types of Questions
- Characteristics of Good Questions
- Guiding Questions by Aims
- How to Frame Good Questions
- What Not to Ask or Question
- Critiquing Your Questioning Technique
- Importance & Benefits of Being a Good Listener
- Why We Don't Listen
- Types/Modes of Listening
- Barriers to Effective Listening
- Degrees/Levels of Active Listening
- The Process of Listening
- Steps to Be an Effective Listener
- Encouraging & Prompting Conversations
- Action Plans and Exercises
- Appendix: Worksheets and Tools for Self-Assessment
- Conclusion: Mastering the Art of Questioning & Listening Skills
- About the Author

Preface

Welcome to the exploration of an essential aspect of human interaction- **'Effective Questioning and Listening Skills'**. In a world inundated with information and constant communication, the ability to ask the right questions and listen actively has become a profound art.

This book is crafted as a guide, a companion on your journey toward mastering the intricacies of communication. Whether you're a professional navigating the complex landscape of the workplace, a student seeking to enhance your learning experience, or an individual striving for more meaningful connections in your personal life, the principles within these pages are designed to empower you.

The Significance of Questioning and Listening: The genesis of this book lies in the recognition of the transformative power of questions and the profound impact of active listening. The ability to inquire thoughtfully and listen attentively transcends mere communication; it is the cornerstone of effective collaboration, understanding, and empathy.

Tailored for Diverse Audiences: This book is not a one-size-fits-all manual. It is tailored for diverse audiences, including but not limited to professionals, educators, students, and anyone seeking to enhance their communication prowess. The principles explored are versatile, applicable in boardrooms, classrooms, living rooms, and every space where human connection flourishes.

A Holistic Exploration: Our journey begins with understanding the audience—identifying unique challenges and demonstrating how improved questioning and listening skills can elevate personal and professional lives. We delve into the purposes of questioning, explore the types of questions, dissect the characteristics of good questions, and guide you through the process of framing questions with precision.

Practical Applications and Real-life Scenarios: Throughout this book, we don't just dwell on theories; we immerse ourselves in practical applications. Real-life scenarios, examples, and action plans are embedded in every chapter. You will find yourself in workplace meetings, family conversations, educational settings, and social gatherings, discovering how to navigate each with finesse.

Continuous Improvement and Action Plans: This journey isn't about perfection but continuous improvement. The appendix offers hands-on tools, worksheets, and self-assessment surveys. It encourages you to engage actively, reflect on your experiences, set goals, and track your progress. The goal is not just to read but to apply, adapt, and evolve.

A Lifelong Skillset: Effective questioning and listening are not just skills; they are a lifelong skillset. As you progress through these pages, envision a future where your questions inspire innovation, your listening fosters understanding, and your communication transforms relationships.

Acknowledgment: I extend heartfelt gratitude to those who contributed directly or indirectly to the creation of this book. The journey of exploration is often a collective effort, and I am thankful for the diverse perspectives that have shaped these pages.

May this book be your guide, your source of inspiration, and your toolkit as you embark on the path to becoming a masterful communicator. Here's to the art of questioning and listening—the profound keys to unlocking the doors of connection and understanding.

Best wishes on your transformative journey.

Understanding the Audience

In the realm of effective communication, the first step is recognizing the diverse audience that can benefit from honing questioning and listening skills. This chapter focuses on identifying the unique communication challenges faced by professionals in various fields, such as doctors, teachers, advocates, and sales professionals.

Identifying the Target Readership: Understanding the specific needs of different professions is crucial. For doctors, effective communication is pivotal in understanding patient symptoms, conveying diagnoses, and ensuring treatment compliance. Teachers require adept questioning and listening skills to engage students, address concerns, and facilitate effective learning. Advocates, in the legal domain, must navigate sensitive conversations with clients and colleagues. Sales professionals, on the other hand, rely on communication to understand client needs and build trust.

Unique Communication Challenges: Each profession brings its set of challenges. Doctors may encounter patients who struggle to articulate symptoms or express anxiety about medical procedures. Teachers may face disengaged students or challenging questions. Advocates often deal with clients navigating legal complexities, and sales professionals encounter diverse client personalities and objections.

Demonstrating Enhancements in Professional and Personal Lives: To illustrate the tangible benefits of improved questioning and listening skills, consider the case of a doctor who learns to ask open-ended questions to better understand a patient's medical history. This not only leads to more accurate diagnoses but also fosters a trusting patient-doctor relationship. A teacher who actively listens to student concerns creates a positive classroom environment, enhancing both academic performance and student well-being.

For advocates, mastering the art of questioning can uncover crucial details in legal cases, while empathetic listening can provide emotional support to clients. Sales professionals employing effective questioning techniques tailor their pitch to address client needs, resulting in increased sales and client satisfaction.

Action Plan for Improvement: Each profession can benefit from tailored action plans. For doctors, this might involve incorporating active listening exercises into medical training, ensuring practitioners can navigate emotional discussions with empathy. Teachers could attend workshops focused on questioning techniques that promote student engagement. Advocates may participate in mock trial scenarios to refine their questioning skills, and sales professionals can engage in role-playing exercises to enhance their ability to ask probing questions and actively listen to client needs.

By the end of this chapter, readers will have gained insights into how questioning and listening skills can be transformative in their specific professional contexts. The subsequent chapters will delve deeper into the mechanics of these skills, providing practical strategies and examples tailored to each profession.

The overarching goal is to equip readers with the tools they need to not only excel in their careers but also enrich their personal lives through meaningful communication.

The Purposes of Questioning

Questioning is a multifaceted skill that serves diverse purposes in communication. In this chapter, we delve into the various goals behind asking questions, illustrating how they are integral to information gathering, problem-solving, and building rapport. Through real-world examples tailored to different professions, readers will gain a nuanced understanding of the strategic use of questions.

Exploring Information Gathering: One primary purpose of questioning is to gather information. Consider a scenario in a medical setting where a doctor seeks to diagnose a patient's symptoms. The doctor's ability to ask precise and relevant questions not only aids in obtaining critical information but also demonstrates a thorough and caring approach. This process is crucial across professions, such as lawyers extracting details from clients, teachers gauging student comprehension, or sales professionals understanding customer needs.

Real-world Example – Sales Professional: A sales professional, keen on understanding a client's requirements, employs open-ended questions to uncover specific challenges and desires. By doing so, they tailor their product pitch to address the client's unique needs, fostering a connection that goes beyond a transactional exchange. This approach not only enhances the sales process but also establishes a foundation for long-term client relationships.

Problem-solving through Questioning: Questions play a pivotal role in problem-solving. In a legal context, an advocate might pose strategic questions during witness examination to build a compelling case. Similarly, a teacher, faced with a class struggling with a concept, can use probing questions to guide students toward a solution. By exploring real-world examples in each profession, readers will grasp the art of using questions as problem-solving tools.

Real-world Example – Teacher: A teacher facing a classroom challenge, such as disengagement or confusion, can employ strategic questions to identify the root cause. Through active listening, the teacher gauges student concerns and tailors their approach to address the specific learning needs of the class. This not only resolves the immediate issue but also fosters a collaborative problem-solving environment within the classroom.

Building Rapport through Questions: Questions are instrumental in building rapport and establishing connections. In professions like sales and healthcare, where trust is paramount, asking empathetic questions creates a more personalized and caring interaction. This holds true for teachers building relationships with students and advocates connecting with clients on a personal level.

Real-world Example – Healthcare Professional: A healthcare professional asking a patient about their well-being beyond the immediate medical concerns demonstrates a genuine interest in the patient's overall health. This not only builds rapport but also contributes to a holistic approach to healthcare. In this chapter, readers will explore how questions can be framed to establish rapport and enhance interpersonal relationships in various professional settings.

Action Plan for Skill Development: Readers will be encouraged to reflect on their own professions and identify scenarios where refining their questioning skills can lead to improved outcomes. Practical exercises and role-playing scenarios are provided to help readers apply the concepts learned in real-world situations. By the end of this chapter, readers will not only understand the purposes of questioning but also have actionable strategies for integrating these skills into their professional toolkit.

Practical Exercises and Actionable Strategies

Here, in this section, we not only explore the various purposes of questioning but also ensure that readers can seamlessly integrate these insights into their professional toolkit. The practical exercises and role-playing scenarios provided are designed to create a hands-on learning experience, fostering a deep understanding of how questioning serves different goals in various contexts.

Practical Exercises:

Goal-Oriented Question Crafting:

- ✓ Objective: Develop the skill of tailoring questions to specific goals.
- ✓ Exercise: Choose a professional scenario (e.g., a team meeting or client interaction) and craft questions that align with different goals, such as information gathering, problem-solving, or building rapport.

Situational Questioning Analysis:

- ✓ Objective: Recognize the most effective types of questions in different situations.
- ✓ Exercise: Analyze case studies or real-world scenarios, identifying the types of questions

that would best serve the objectives in each context.

Questioning in Problem-Solving Scenarios:
- ✓ Objective: Apply questioning techniques to solve workplace challenges.
- ✓ Exercise: Present a workplace problem or challenge, and devise a series of questions that would lead to a comprehensive understanding and potential solutions.

Role-Playing Scenarios:

Client Consultation Role-Play:
- ✓ Objective: Practice asking probing questions to understand client needs.
- ✓ Scenario: Simulate a client consultation where the reader takes on the role of a professional, asking questions to uncover client requirements and expectations.

Team Collaboration Simulation:
- ✓ Objective: Enhance collaboration through effective questioning.
- ✓ Scenario: Role-play a team meeting, incorporating open-ended questions to encourage team members to share ideas, perspectives, and potential solutions.

Actionable Strategies:

Question Patterning Technique:
- ✓ Strategy: Develop a set of go-to question patterns for different purposes (e.g., open-ended questions for exploration, closed-ended for confirmation).
- ✓ Implementation: Practice using these patterns in various scenarios to reinforce versatility.

Goal-Alignment Framework:
- ✓ Strategy: Align questioning strategies with overarching goals.

✓ Implementation: Develop a framework that connects specific questioning techniques to broader professional objectives. Apply this framework in day-to-day interactions.

Continuous Reflection and Adjustment:

✓ Strategy: Regularly reflect on the effectiveness of questions posed.

✓ Implementation: After significant interactions, reflect on the questions used and their impact. Adjust strategies based on reflections for continuous improvement.

By engaging in these exercises and implementing the actionable strategies, readers will not only comprehend the multifaceted purposes of questioning but also acquire the practical skills necessary to wield questions effectively in their professional endeavors. The integration of theoretical knowledge with hands-on practice positions readers to become adept and strategic communicators in a variety of settings.

Types of Questions

Questions are not one-size-fits-all; they come in various types, each serving a unique purpose. In this chapter, we explore the nuances of different question types, from open-ended to closed-ended, probing, reflective, and leading questions. By understanding when and how to use each type, readers will gain a comprehensive toolkit for effective communication.

Distinguishing Between Open-ended and Closed-ended Questions: Open-ended questions invite expansive responses, encouraging the speaker to provide detailed information and share thoughts and feelings. In contrast, closed-ended questions elicit brief, specific answers. For instance, a doctor might use open-ended questions to understand a patient's overall health, while closed-ended questions could be employed to gather specific medical history details.

Real-world Example – Doctor's Appointment: During a doctor's appointment, an open-ended question like, "Can you describe any symptoms you've been experiencing?" encourages the patient to share details freely. On the other hand, a closed-ended question such as, "Have you experienced nausea in the past week?" aims to gather specific information for diagnosis.

Discussing Probing Questions: Probing questions are designed to delve deeper into a topic, encouraging the speaker to elaborate on their initial response. In a sales context, a sales professional may use probing questions to understand a client's objections more thoroughly, uncovering the root cause.

Real-world Example – Sales Professional: A sales professional, faced with a hesitant client, might ask a probing question like, "Could you help me understand what specific concerns you have about our product?" This encourages the client to express their reservations, providing valuable insights that can be addressed effectively.

Reflective Questions for Thoughtful Responses: Reflective questions prompt individuals to contemplate their thoughts and experiences. In a teaching scenario, a reflective question can be used to encourage students to consider alternative perspectives or think critically about a subject.

Real-world Example – Teacher in a Literature Class: A literature teacher, discussing a novel, might pose a reflective question like, "How do you think the protagonist's choices reflect the societal norms of that era?" This type of question encourages students to analyze the text on a deeper level, fostering critical thinking.

Leading Questions to Guide the Conversation: Leading questions subtly guide the conversation in a particular direction. In a legal setting, an advocate might use leading questions during cross-examination to influence the witness's narrative.

Real-world Example – Legal Cross-examination: An advocate cross-examining a witness may ask a leading question like, "Wouldn't you agree that the defendant's actions were reckless?" This shapes the narrative in a way that aligns with the advocate's argument.

Action Plan for Skill Development: To enhance their questioning skills, readers will be encouraged to practice formulating both open-ended and closed-ended questions in various scenarios relevant to their professions. Role-playing exercises will help them experiment with probing, reflective, and leading questions.

By the end of this chapter, readers will have a nuanced understanding of question types and the ability to strategically employ them to achieve desired communication outcomes in their respective fields.

Types of Questions - Practical Application

This section is dedicated to honing the skill of formulating different types of questions. The goal is to empower readers with the ability to strategically choose between open-ended and closed-ended questions in diverse professional scenarios. Through practical exercises, readers will gain a nuanced understanding of when to use each type effectively.

Practical Application:

Open-Ended Question Formulation:

- ✓ Objective: Develop the art of crafting open-ended questions that encourage detailed responses and stimulate thoughtful discussion.
- ✓ Exercise: Select a professional scenario (e.g., a client meeting, team brainstorming session) and formulate open-ended questions that prompt participants to share insights, ideas, and opinions.
- ✓ *Example:* Instead of asking, *"Did the project meet your expectations?"* try, *"What aspects of the project exceeded or fell short of your expectations, and why?"*

Closed-Ended Question Formulation:

- ✓ Objective: Master the skill of using closed-ended questions for precise information gathering and confirmation.

- ✓ Exercise: Imagine scenarios where specific information is needed (e.g., in a medical consultation or during a project status update). Formulate closed-ended questions to efficiently gather the required details.
- ✓ *Example:* Instead of asking, *"Tell me about the challenges you faced,"* try, *"Were there any specific challenges related to the project timeline that you encountered?"*

Combination Exercise:
- ✓ Objective: Practice seamlessly transitioning between open-ended and closed-ended questions in a conversation.
- ✓ Exercise: Simulate a conversation related to your profession. Start with open-ended questions to encourage sharing, then strategically shift to closed-ended questions for clarification or confirmation.
- ✓ *Example:* Begin with, *"Can you share your overall experience with the project?"* and transition to, *"Did the team face any obstacles during the implementation phase?"*

Scenario-Specific Examples:

Sales Professional Scenario:
- ✓ *Open-Ended Question:* "How would you describe your current experience with our product or service?"
- ✓ *Closed-Ended Question:* "Have you previously used a similar product from one of our competitors?"

Educator/Teacher Scenario:
- ✓ *Open-Ended Question:* "What are some innovative teaching methods you've found effective in engaging students?"

- ✓ *Closed-Ended Question:* "Did you implement any specific teaching strategies to address student participation in your last class?"

Medical Professional Scenario:

- ✓ *Open-Ended Question:* "Can you describe the symptoms you've been experiencing recently?"
- ✓ *Closed-Ended Question:* "Have you had any allergies or adverse reactions to medications in the past?"

By engaging in these exercises and utilizing the provided examples, readers will not only grasp the distinction between open-ended and closed-ended questions but also gain the practical expertise to employ each type strategically in their professional contexts. This hands-on application ensures that the knowledge acquired in this chapter becomes a tangible skill set, enhancing the effectiveness of their communication in various professional scenarios.

Characteristics of Good Questions

The art of questioning extends beyond the type of question asked; it involves crafting questions with specific characteristics that elicit meaningful responses. In this chapter, we delve into the key characteristics of good questions, emphasizing clarity, relevance, precision, and their role in encouraging critical thinking and thoughtful responses.

Clarity in Questioning: Good questions are clear and unambiguous, leaving no room for misinterpretation. Whether in a classroom, a sales pitch, or a medical consultation, clarity ensures that the respondent understands the intended inquiry. For example, a teacher might ask a clear question like, "Can you explain the main theme of the assigned reading?" This clarity enables students to provide focused and relevant responses.

Relevance as a Guiding Principle: Relevance is a crucial characteristic of good questions, ensuring that they align with the context and purpose of the conversation. In a sales context, asking relevant questions about a client's specific needs demonstrates an understanding of their requirements, building rapport and trust.

Real-world Example – Sales Professional: A sales professional inquiring about a client's business goals before proposing a solution ensures the questions are relevant to the client's objectives. This not only showcases the salesperson's attentiveness but also establishes a foundation for a tailored and impactful pitch.

Precision for Specific Insights: Precise questions are crafted with a specific focus, seeking targeted information. In the medical field, a precise question might be, "Can you describe the onset and duration of your symptoms?" This precision aids in accurate diagnosis and treatment planning.

Real-world Example – Doctor's Consultation: A doctor asking a patient precisely about the symptoms' timeline and characteristics helps narrow down potential causes, guiding the diagnostic process effectively.

Encouraging Critical Thinking through Questions: Good questions go beyond seeking information; they stimulate critical thinking. In an educational setting, a teacher might pose a question that challenges students to analyze, evaluate, and synthesize information.

Real-world Example – Classroom Scenario: A teacher asking, "How would the historical events we discussed impact society today?" encourages students to think critically about the relevance of historical knowledge, fostering a deeper understanding of the subject matter.

Crafting Questions for Thoughtful Responses: Good questions are designed to elicit thoughtful and reflective responses. In therapeutic settings, therapists often use carefully crafted questions to guide clients in exploring their emotions and experiences.

Real-world Example – Therapeutic Session: A therapist asking, "Can you describe a time when you felt differently about this situation?" prompts the client to reflect on their emotions and gain insights into their own thought processes.

Action Plan for Skill Development: Readers will engage in exercises aimed at crafting clear, relevant, and precise questions tailored to their professional contexts. Additionally, they will be encouraged to design questions that stimulate critical thinking and thoughtful responses. Through role-playing scenarios and real-world applications, readers will refine their ability to create questions that not only extract information but also contribute to the depth and quality of the conversation.

By honing the characteristics of good questions, readers will not only become more adept communicators but also contribute to a more meaningful and impactful exchange of ideas in both professional and personal spheres. The subsequent chapters will further build on these skills, providing readers with a holistic approach to effective questioning and communication.

Characteristics of Good Questions - Ensuring Effectiveness in Questioning

Understanding the characteristics of good questions is fundamental to effective communication. This section focuses on delineating these characteristics and providing guidance on how to ensure they are maintained during the questioning process. By mastering these traits, readers will elevate their ability to pose insightful and impactful questions in diverse professional settings.

Characteristics of Good Questions:

Clarity:

> ✓ *Guidance:* Clearly articulate the question to avoid ambiguity.

- ✓ *Example:* Instead of a vague inquiry like *"How's it going?"* ask, *"Can you share the progress made on the project milestones this week?"*

Relevance:
- ✓ *Guidance:* Align questions with the context and goals of the conversation.
- ✓ *Example:* In a marketing meeting, ask, *"How does this campaign strategy contribute to our overall brand positioning?"*

Precision:
- ✓ *Guidance:* Formulate questions with precision to elicit specific information.
- ✓ *Example:* Instead of a broad query like *"Tell me about the client meeting,"* ask, *"What were the key client concerns raised during the meeting, and how do we plan to address them?"*

Conciseness:
- ✓ *Guidance:* Keep questions concise and to the point.
- ✓ *Example:* Instead of a lengthy inquiry, *"Can you give me a detailed breakdown of your approach to solving this problem?"* ask, *"What's your strategy for addressing this issue?"*

Openness:
- ✓ *Guidance:* Foster an open atmosphere that encourages honest and unrestrained responses.
- ✓ *Example:* Use open-ended questions like *"Can you share your perspective on the recent project challenges?"*

Non-Bias:

✓ *Guidance:* Frame questions impartially to avoid leading or influencing responses.
✓ *Example:* Instead of a biased question like *"Don't you think the current process is inefficient?"* ask, *"What are your thoughts on the efficiency of the current process?"*

Maintaining Characteristics During Questioning:
Preparation:
✓ *Guidance:* Before engaging in a conversation, outline key questions based on the characteristics outlined.
✓ *Example:* Outline questions for a client meeting, ensuring they are clear, relevant, and concise.

Active Listening:
✓ *Guidance:* Adjust follow-up questions based on the responses received, demonstrating active listening.
✓ *Example:* If a team member mentions unexpected challenges, follow up with a precise question like *"Can you elaborate on the specific challenges faced and potential solutions?"*

Flexibility:
✓ *Guidance:* Be flexible in adjusting your questioning approach based on the dynamics of the conversation.
✓ *Example:* If a closed-ended question initially yields limited information, adapt by posing an open-ended follow-up question.

Reflective Practice:
Guidance: Regularly review past interactions, assessing the effectiveness of questions posed.

Example: Reflect on a recent client meeting and evaluate whether your questions aligned with the characteristics discussed in this chapter.

By consciously incorporating these characteristics into their questioning approach and employing the provided guidance, readers will ensure that their questions are clear, relevant, precise, and conducive to open and unbiased dialogue. This chapter serves as a practical guide, equipping readers with the tools to consistently pose questions that contribute to meaningful and productive conversations in their professional endeavors.

Guiding Questions by Aims

The effectiveness of questioning lies not just in the type and characteristics of questions but also in aligning them with specific goals. In this chapter, we explore how questions can be strategically tailored to achieve distinct aims. Whether the goal is information gathering, relationship-building, or problem-solving, understanding this aspect of questioning is crucial for communicators across diverse professions.

Understanding Tailored Questions for Specific Goals: Questions are versatile tools that can be wielded with precision based on the desired outcome. This chapter delves into the art of aligning questions with specific goals, emphasizing how thoughtful questioning can be a strategic asset in various professional contexts.

Examples of Goal-Oriented Questioning in Different Contexts:

Goal: Information Gathering (Legal Profession) In a legal setting, an advocate might employ questions aimed at gathering specific details to build a compelling case. For instance, asking a witness, *"Can you provide a detailed account of the events leading up to the incident?"* serves the goal of extracting relevant information crucial for legal proceedings.

Goal: Relationship-Building (Sales Profession) In sales, where relationship-building is paramount, a sales professional might ask questions focused on understanding the client's business and needs. For instance, *"What are the key challenges your company is currently facing?"* positions the salesperson as a strategic partner, actively engaged in the client's success.

Goal: Problem-Solving (Education Profession) In an educational context, teachers often use questions to guide students through problem-solving processes. For instance, a science teacher might ask, *"How can we design an experiment to test this hypothesis?"* This type of questioning fosters critical thinking and encourages students to apply their knowledge to real-world scenarios.

Goal: Building Rapport (Healthcare Profession) In healthcare, building rapport is essential for effective patient care. A healthcare professional might ask questions aimed at understanding the patient's concerns and experiences. For example, *"Can you share any specific fears or anxieties you have about the upcoming procedure?"* demonstrates empathy and fosters a trusting patient-professional relationship.

Action Plan for Tailoring Questions to Goals: Readers will engage in exercises designed to align questions with specific goals relevant to their professions. Through role-playing scenarios, they will practice crafting questions that serve distinct purposes, whether it be information gathering, relationship-building, or problem-solving. This hands-on approach will empower readers to apply these skills in their day-to-day interactions.

By mastering the art of tailoring questions to specific goals, readers will elevate their communication skills to a strategic level. The subsequent chapters will further build on this foundation, providing readers with a holistic understanding of questioning and communication, ultimately empowering them to navigate diverse professional scenarios with finesse and purpose.

Guiding Questions by Aims - Tailoring Questions to Goals

This section dives into the strategic aspect of questioning—aligning questions with specific goals. Readers will not only understand the nuances of tailoring questions but also engage in practical exercises, including role-playing scenarios. By the end, readers will possess a skill set to craft purpose-driven questions for diverse professional aims.

Action Plan for Tailoring Questions to Goals:

Identifying Professional Goals:

- ✓ *Exercise:* Reflect on current professional objectives.
- ✓ *Example:* A sales professional may aim to understand client needs, an educator may seek to enhance student engagement, and a project manager may focus on problem-solving within the team.

Goal-Specific Question Crafting:

- ✓ *Exercise:* Craft questions tailored to specific professional goals.
- ✓ *Example Template: Goal:* Enhancing Client Relationships
- ✓ *Question: "Can you share your experience with our services and highlight aspects you find most valuable?"*

Role-Playing Scenarios:

- ✓ *Exercise:* Engage in role-playing scenarios relevant to professional aims.
- ✓ *Example Scenario: Goal:* Information Gathering for Project Management

✓ *Role Play:* Simulate a team meeting where you, as the project manager, pose questions to gather crucial information on project status, potential obstacles, and team dynamics.

Problem-Solving Through Questions:

✓ *Exercise:* Use questions as problem-solving tools.

✓ *Example Template: Goal:* Addressing Workplace Challenges

✓ *Question: "What specific steps can we take to overcome the current challenges in meeting project deadlines?"*

Relationship-Building Through Inquiry:

✓ *Exercise:* Craft questions to foster relationships.

✓ *Example Template: Goal:* Building Stronger Team Bonds

✓ *Question: "How can we enhance collaboration and communication within the team to ensure a more cohesive working environment?"*

Feedback-Seeking Questions:

✓ *Exercise:* Develop questions to seek constructive feedback.

✓ *Example Template: Goal:* Continuous Professional Development

✓ *Question: "What suggestions do you have for improving our team's collaborative efforts, and how can I contribute to this improvement?"*

Role-Playing Scenario Example:

Professional Goal: Enhancing Client Relationships

✓ *Scenario:* Imagine you are a sales professional meeting with a long-term client. Your goal is to strengthen the relationship and uncover opportunities for further collaboration.

✓ *Role Play:* Initiate the conversation with an open-ended question: *"How has your experience been with our products/services so far?"* Depending on the response, follow up with specific inquiries tailored to their feedback, needs, and potential areas of improvement.

Through these exercises and examples, readers will not only grasp the theory of aligning questions with goals but also gain practical proficiency. The templates provided serve as starting points for crafting purpose-driven questions, ensuring that readers can seamlessly integrate this skill into their professional toolkit, fostering better relationships, problem-solving, and overall success in their respective fields.

How to Frame Good Questions

While the importance of asking good questions is undeniable, mastering the art of question framing requires more than just an understanding of types and characteristics. This chapter delves into the practical aspects of constructing effective questions, providing valuable insights, tips, and exercises to enhance question-posing skills.

Practical Tips for Constructing Effective Questions: Framing effective questions is a skill that can be honed with practical tips. One key tip is to start questions with interrogative words like "what," "how," "why," or "can." These words open the door to detailed responses, encouraging the respondent to share more than a simple yes or no. For example, instead of asking, *"Did you like the presentation?"* a more effective question could be, *"What aspects of the presentation resonated with you, and why?"*

Another tip is to keep questions concise and focused. Clarity is lost in lengthy inquiries, and respondents may become overwhelmed. The goal is to guide the conversation without overwhelming or confusing the other party.

Avoiding Common Pitfalls in Question Formulation: While constructing questions, it's crucial to avoid common pitfalls that can hinder effective communication. One common pitfall is the use of ambiguous language. Ambiguous questions can lead to confusion and inaccurate responses. For instance, asking, *"Could you maybe explain that a bit?"* lacks specificity and may not yield the desired information.

Another pitfall is the inclusion of assumptions in questions. Assumptions can bias responses and limit the breadth of information gathered. For instance, asking, *"How did you feel about the decision, given its obvious flaws?"* assumes the decision has obvious flaws, potentially influencing the respondent's answer.

Exercises to Enhance Question-Posing Skills: To reinforce the principles discussed, readers will engage in practical exercises designed to enhance their question-posing skills. These exercises may involve crafting questions for hypothetical scenarios, role-playing, or analyzing and refining existing questions. The goal is to provide a hands-on approach that allows readers to apply the concepts learned in real-world contexts.

Real-world Example – Business Negotiation: Consider a business negotiation scenario where clarity is paramount. Instead of asking, *"Are you okay with the proposed terms?"* a more effective question might be, *"How do the proposed terms align with your business objectives, and are there any adjustments you would suggest?"*

Action Plan for Skill Development: Readers will be encouraged to assess their own question-posing skills by reflecting on past interactions and identifying areas for improvement. The action plan will involve setting specific goals for question formulation, practicing in various professional contexts, and seeking feedback from peers or mentors.

By providing practical tips, highlighting common pitfalls, and offering exercises for skill development, this chapter aims to equip readers with the tools needed to frame good questions effectively. As readers progress through the subsequent chapters, they will have a solid foundation to not only understand the theory behind effective questioning but also implement these skills in their professional and personal interactions.

How to Frame Good Questions - Skill Development Action Plan

This section focuses on the practical aspect of framing good questions. The action plan outlined here will guide readers through a self-assessment of their question-posing skills, encouraging reflection, goal-setting, and hands-on practice in professional contexts. The goal is to empower readers to refine their question formulation skills systematically.

Action Plan for Skill Development:

Self-Assessment of Question-Posing Skills:

- ✓ *Exercise:* Reflect on recent interactions involving question-posing.
- ✓ *Example Template: Situation:* A team meeting to discuss a project.
- ✓ *Reflection: "I noticed that my questions were predominantly closed-ended. This limited the depth of the discussion."*

Identifying Areas for Improvement:

- ✓ *Exercise:* Identify specific areas for improvement based on self-assessment.
- ✓ *Example Template: Area for Improvement:* Incorporating more open-ended questions to stimulate discussion and gather diverse perspectives.

Setting Specific Goals for Question Formulation:

- ✓ *Exercise:* Establish clear and measurable goals for question formulation.

- ✓ *Example Template: Goal:* Increase the use of open-ended questions by 20% in team meetings over the next month.

Practicing in Various Professional Contexts:
- ✓ *Exercise:* Apply the set goals in real-world professional scenarios.
- ✓ *Example Scenario: Professional Context:* Leading a client consultation.
- ✓ *Practice Goal:* Pose at least three open-ended questions to understand the client's needs and expectations thoroughly.

Seeking Feedback from Peers or Mentors:
- ✓ *Exercise:* Actively seek feedback on question-posing skills.
- ✓ *Example Template: Feedback Request: "I'm working on improving my question-posing skills, particularly in making questions more open-ended. Can you provide feedback on how I handled questions in our recent team meeting?"*

Continuous Review and Adjustment:
- ✓ *Exercise:* Regularly review interactions, adjusting strategies based on feedback.
- ✓ *Example Template: Review:* After each client interaction, assess the effectiveness of questions used and adjust future strategies accordingly.

Example Reflection and Goal-Setting:
- ✓ *Reflection:* In a recent project discussion, I observed that my questions were often too focused on seeking confirmation rather than exploring alternative solutions or gathering diverse opinions.
- ✓ *Goal-Setting:* Increase the diversity of question types in project discussions by

incorporating at least one probing question in each meeting over the next month.

Feedback Request Template:

Subject: Seeking Feedback on Questioning Skills

Message: Dear [Peer/Mentor's Name],

I hope this message finds you well. I am actively working on enhancing my question-posing skills, particularly in making questions more open-ended to stimulate better discussions. I would greatly appreciate your feedback on how I handled questions in our recent team meeting. Your insights will be invaluable in my growth.

Thank you in advance for taking the time.

Best regards, [Your Name]

By engaging in this action plan, readers will not only assess and improve their question-posing skills but also cultivate a habit of continuous improvement. The provided templates offer structured guidance for self-reflection, goal-setting, and seeking constructive feedback, ensuring that readers actively apply and refine their question formulation skills in diverse professional contexts.

Examples of Questioning in Different Settings

Questioning is a universal skill that transcends professional boundaries, influencing various aspects of our lives. This chapter explores questioning techniques in diverse settings such as home, workplace, school, college, and social situations. Real-life scenarios and examples will illuminate the application of effective questioning in these contexts, providing readers with a practical understanding of how to navigate different scenarios.

Questioning at Home: Effective questioning at home is crucial for fostering understanding and maintaining healthy relationships. In family discussions, a parent might use open-ended questions to encourage children to express their feelings or thoughts. For instance, asking, *"Can you tell me about your day?"* allows for a more in-depth conversation than a closed-ended question like, *"Did you have a good day?"*

Real-life Scenario – Family Decision-making: Consider a scenario where a family is making decisions about a vacation destination. A well-crafted question like, *"What experiences are important for each of us during the vacation?"* invites input from each family member, contributing to a more inclusive decision-making process.

Questioning in the Workplace: In a professional setting, questioning becomes a powerful tool for collaboration, problem-solving, and decision-making. A manager might use probing questions during a team meeting to uncover potential challenges or innovative ideas. For instance, asking, *"What obstacles do you foresee in implementing this strategy?"* encourages team members to think critically and contribute valuable insights.

Real-life Scenario – Team Collaboration: Imagine a workplace scenario where a team is working on a project. A reflective question like, *"How can we improve our collaboration to meet project deadlines more efficiently?"* prompts team members to assess their working dynamics and propose constructive solutions.

Questioning in an Educational Setting: Teachers employ questioning as a core pedagogical tool to stimulate student engagement, critical thinking, and knowledge retention. In a classroom, a teacher might use leading questions to guide students toward a specific concept. For example, asking, *"What do you think the author intended to convey in this passage?"* encourages students to analyze and interpret the text.

Real-life Scenario – Classroom Discussion: During a literature class, a teacher might pose an open-ended question like, *"How do the characters' choices influence the plot?"* This question prompts students to explore the narrative's intricacies, fostering a deeper understanding of the literary work.

Questioning in a Social Setting: In social situations, effective questioning contributes to meaningful conversations and relationship-building. For instance, at a social gathering, one might use open-ended questions to learn more about others. Asking, *"What sparked your interest in that hobby?"* creates an opportunity for a more personal and enriching exchange compared to closed-ended inquiries.

Real-life Scenario – Networking Event: Consider a networking event where individuals are meeting for the first time. A relevant and open-ended question like, *"What inspired you to pursue your current career path?"* not only facilitates conversation but also establishes a foundation for genuine connections.

Action Plan for Application: Readers will be encouraged to reflect on their own experiences in these settings, identifying opportunities to enhance their questioning skills. The action plan involves setting specific goals for incorporating effective questioning techniques in different contexts, practicing these skills, and reflecting on the outcomes.

By exploring real-life scenarios in various settings, readers gain a practical understanding of how questioning techniques can be adapted to different environments. As readers progress through the subsequent chapters, they will be equipped to apply these insights in their personal and professional lives, fostering effective communication and relationship-building in diverse settings.

Examples of Questioning in Different Settings - Application Action Plan

This section focuses on real-life examples of questioning in various settings. The action plan outlined here encourages readers to reflect on their own experiences, identify opportunities for improvement, and actively incorporate effective questioning techniques into different contexts. The goal is to make the theoretical knowledge applicable in practical scenarios.

Action Plan for Application:

Reflection on Personal Experiences:

- ✓ *Exercise:* Reflect on recent experiences in different settings (e.g., workplace, social gatherings, family discussions) where questions played a role.
- ✓ *Example Template: Setting:* Workplace meeting.
- ✓ *Reflection: "In the last team meeting, I noticed that my questions focused mainly on progress updates. There were missed opportunities to delve deeper into team dynamics and individual contributions."*

Identifying Opportunities for Enhancement:

- ✓ *Exercise:* Identify specific opportunities for enhancing questioning skills in each setting.

- ✓ *Example Template: Setting:* Family dinner.
- ✓ *Opportunity: "During family discussions, I often default to closed-ended questions. I can improve by incorporating more open-ended inquiries to encourage everyone's participation."*

Setting Specific Goals for Questioning Techniques:
- ✓ *Exercise:* Set clear and measurable goals for incorporating effective questioning techniques.
- ✓ *Example Template: Setting:* Social gatherings.
- ✓ *Goal:* Pose at least two open-ended questions in each social gathering to deepen conversations and connect with others on a more meaningful level.

Practicing Effective Questioning Skills:
- ✓ *Exercise:* Actively practice the identified questioning techniques in different contexts.
- ✓ *Example Scenario: Professional Context:* During team discussions, practice asking probing questions to explore team dynamics and individual contributions beyond surface-level updates.

Reflection on Outcomes:
- ✓ *Exercise:* Reflect on the outcomes of applying effective questioning techniques.
- ✓ *Example Template: Setting:* Workplace project discussion.
- ✓ *Reflection: "By incorporating open-ended questions, I observed a more engaged and collaborative team discussion. Team members shared valuable insights, and we identified potential improvements in our project approach."*

Example Reflection and Goal-Setting:
- ✓ *Reflection:* In a recent social gathering, I realized that my questions were primarily closed-ended, leading to short and surface-level conversations.
- ✓ *Goal-Setting:* For the next social gathering, set a goal to ask at least three open-ended questions that encourage deeper discussions and connection with others.

By engaging in this action plan, readers will not only understand the importance of effective questioning in different settings but also actively apply this knowledge in their daily interactions. The provided templates offer a structured approach to self-reflection, goal-setting, and outcome assessment, ensuring that readers can enhance their questioning skills systematically in diverse contexts.

What Not to Ask or Question

While effective questioning is essential for meaningful communication, it is equally important to recognize the boundaries and ethical considerations that surround the act of questioning. This chapter focuses on what not to ask or question, emphasizing the identification of sensitive topics, cultural considerations, and the adherence to ethical guidelines.

Identifying Sensitive Topics: Certain topics are inherently sensitive, and probing into these areas without caution can lead to discomfort, offense, or emotional distress. It is crucial to be aware of the emotional and psychological impact of questions related to personal health, finances, relationships, and other private matters.

Example – Health-Related Inquiry: Inquiring about someone's health in a casual setting might seem innocent, but probing into specific medical conditions without consent can be intrusive. A question like, *"Have you been to the doctor for that issue?"* might be inappropriate, especially if the person has not volunteered such information.

Cultural Considerations in Questioning: Cultural differences play a significant role in shaping communication norms. Questions that might be acceptable in one culture could be considered intrusive or offensive in another. Understanding and respecting these cultural nuances is essential to avoid unintended misunderstandings or discomfort.

Example – Personal Relationships: In some cultures, asking about someone's marital status or family planning may be perceived as normal and friendly. However, in cultures where such matters are considered private, these questions can be inappropriate and intrusive.

Ethical Guidelines for Questioning: Ethics form the foundation of responsible questioning. It is essential to adhere to ethical principles, ensuring that questions are posed with integrity, respect, and a commitment to the well-being of the individuals involved. This includes obtaining informed consent when discussing sensitive topics.

Example – Employment Interviews: In a job interview, asking about an applicant's age, marital status, or religious beliefs is not only ethically questionable but may also be illegal in many jurisdictions. Instead, questions should focus on relevant qualifications and experiences related to the job.

Action Plan for Ethical Questioning: Readers will engage in exercises to analyze and categorize questions based on their potential sensitivity and ethical implications. Through case studies and role-playing scenarios, readers will develop a heightened awareness of ethical considerations in questioning.

This chapter serves as a guide to navigate the delicate balance between curiosity and respect, helping readers understand what not to ask or question in various situations. By incorporating cultural sensitivity and ethical guidelines into their questioning practices, readers will not only avoid potential pitfalls but also contribute to fostering a more inclusive and respectful communication environment. The subsequent chapters will further build on these principles, providing readers with a comprehensive understanding of ethical communication practices.

What Not to Ask or Question - Ethical Questioning Action Plan

This section delves into the sensitive aspect of questioning by highlighting what not to ask or question. The action plan outlined here encourages readers to analyze and categorize questions based on their potential sensitivity and ethical implications. Through case studies and role-playing scenarios, readers will develop heightened awareness and a principled approach to ethical considerations in questioning.

Action Plan for Ethical Questioning:

Analysis and Categorization of Questions:

- ✓ *Exercise:* Analyze sample questions and categorize them based on potential sensitivity and ethical implications.
- ✓ *Example Template: Question: "Are you planning to have children soon?"*
- ✓ *Categorization:* Sensitive and potentially invasive.

Case Studies on Ethical Dilemmas:

- ✓ *Exercise:* Engage in case studies that present ethical dilemmas in questioning.
- ✓ *Example Scenario: Case Study:* A hiring manager asking about a candidate's marital status during a job interview.
- ✓ *Analysis:* Discuss the potential ethical concerns and implications of such a question.

Role-Playing Scenarios:

- ✓ *Exercise:* Participate in role-playing scenarios that simulate ethical questioning dilemmas.
- ✓ *Example Scenario: Role Play:* Simulate a doctor-patient consultation where the patient's

religious beliefs may impact treatment decisions. Practice asking questions that respect privacy and uphold ethical standards.

Development of Ethical Guidelines:
- ✓ *Exercise:* Collaboratively develop ethical guidelines for questioning in various settings.
- ✓ *Example Template: Setting:* Workplace team interactions.
- ✓ *Guideline: "Avoid questions related to personal matters that are not directly relevant to work tasks or responsibilities."*

Reflection on Ethical Awareness:

Exercise: Reflect on personal ethical awareness in past questioning situations.
- ✓ *Example Template: Situation:* A client meeting where personal details were inadvertently questioned.
- ✓ *Reflection: "I now realize that I should have been more cautious about probing into personal matters. In the future, I will be more mindful of maintaining ethical boundaries."*

Example Case Study Analysis:
- ✓ *Case Study:* A teacher asking students about their family background in a classroom setting.
- ✓ *Analysis:* This question may be perceived as sensitive, potentially making students uncomfortable. It raises ethical concerns about privacy and the appropriateness of such inquiries in an academic setting.

By actively engaging in the outlined action plan, readers will not only become aware of potential ethical pitfalls in questioning but also develop strategies to navigate such situations responsibly. The examples and templates provided offer practical insights into maintaining ethical boundaries, ensuring that readers approach questioning with sensitivity and respect for ethical considerations in diverse contexts.

Critiquing Your Questioning Technique

Continuous improvement is a hallmark of effective communication. In this chapter, we delve into the art of self-assessment for evaluating one's questioning skills. By providing self-assessment tools, strategies for reflection, and actionable steps for improvement, readers will gain the tools to refine and enhance their questioning techniques over time.

Self-Assessment Tools: Effective self-assessment begins with the development of tools that allow individuals to critically evaluate their questioning techniques. These tools may include reflective questionnaires, scenario analyses, or even video recordings of interpersonal interactions. By objectively examining one's questioning style, strengths, and areas for improvement, individuals can gain valuable insights into their communication dynamics.

Example – Reflective Questionnaire: A reflective questionnaire could include prompts such as:

- ✓ *Did I use a variety of question types in my recent interactions?*
- ✓ *Were my questions clear and concise, or did they lead to confusion?*
- ✓ *Did I adapt my questioning style based on the context and the individual I was communicating with?*

Strategies for Continuous Improvement: Continuous improvement involves an ongoing commitment to refining one's skills based on feedback and self-reflection. Strategies for improvement can encompass a range of actions, from seeking feedback from peers or mentors to engaging in targeted skill-building exercises.

Example – Feedback Seeking: After a client meeting, a sales professional might seek feedback from the client by asking, "Can you share your thoughts on the effectiveness of our communication during this meeting?" This not only demonstrates a commitment to improvement but also provides valuable insights for refining future interactions.

Action Plan for Skill Enhancement: To facilitate skill enhancement, readers will be guided through the development of a personalized action plan. This plan may involve setting specific goals for improvement, scheduling regular self-assessment sessions, and incorporating targeted exercises into daily communication practices.

Example – Goal Setting: A professional aiming to enhance their questioning skills might set a specific goal, such as using reflective questions in at least two client interactions per week. Regularly assessing the effectiveness of these questions and adjusting the approach based on feedback becomes an integral part of the improvement process.

Real-life Scenario – Role-playing Exercises: Engaging in role-playing exercises, either individually or with a partner, provides a safe space to practice and refine questioning techniques. For instance, a teacher looking to improve their use of probing questions might simulate a classroom scenario, experimenting with different approaches and gauging the impact on student engagement.

By embracing the process of self-assessment and committing to continuous improvement, readers will position themselves on a trajectory of growth in their questioning skills. This chapter serves as a guide for readers to not only critique their questioning techniques effectively but also to develop a proactive and intentional approach to ongoing development. As readers progress through the subsequent chapters, they will be equipped to apply these principles in a systematic manner, ensuring a sustained and impactful enhancement of their communication abilities.

Critiquing Your Questioning Technique - Self-Assessment Tools

This section focuses on effective self-assessment tools to empower readers to critically evaluate their questioning techniques. The provided examples and templates offer structured guidance, allowing individuals to analyze their questioning approaches and identify areas for improvement.

Self-Assessment Tools:

Questioning Style Inventory:
- ✓ *Objective:* Assess your predominant questioning style.
- ✓ *Template: Scale:* Rate the frequency of closed-ended versus open-ended questions in recent interactions.
- ✓ *Reflection: "I notice a tendency to rely more on closed-ended questions. Exploring ways to incorporate open-ended inquiries would enhance the depth of my conversations."*

Goal Alignment Checklist:
- ✓ *Objective:* Evaluate the alignment of your questions with specific goals.
- ✓ *Template: List:* Identify recent professional goals.

- ✓ *Checklist:* Evaluate questions posed in relation to each goal.
- ✓ *Reflection:* *"While discussing project milestones, my questions were too focused on progress updates. Next time, I'll incorporate more probing questions to gather diverse insights."*

Reflective Questioning Journal:
- ✓ *Objective:* Maintain a journal for reflective questioning practices.
- ✓ *Template: Entry:* Document key questions posed in recent interactions.
- ✓ *Reflection:* Analyze the effectiveness of each question and note areas for improvement.
- ✓ *Action Plan:* Set goals for refining questioning techniques based on reflections.

Diversity of Question Types Analysis:
- ✓ *Objective:* Assess the diversity of question types used.
- ✓ *Template: Categories:* List categories of questions (open-ended, closed-ended, probing, reflective).
- ✓ *Frequency Analysis:* Record the frequency of each question type in recent interactions.
- ✓ *Insights:* Identify patterns and areas for diversifying question types.

Impact Assessment Grid:
- ✓ *Objective:* Evaluate the impact of questions on the conversation.
- ✓ *Template: Grid:* Create a grid with columns for different questions and rows for their impact (e.g., stimulating, clarifying, leading).
- ✓ *Analysis:* Assess the overall impact of questions used in recent discussions.

✓ *Adjustment Plan:* Identify areas for adjusting question types based on impact.

Example Reflective Questioning Journal Entry:

Date: [Date]

Interaction Summary: Team meeting to discuss project updates.

Key Questions Posed:

✓ *"How is the project progressing?"*

✓ *"Did we encounter any challenges?"*

✓ *"Can you elaborate on the client's feedback?"*

Reflection:

✓ Question 1: Closed-ended, limited insights. Consider more open-ended queries.

✓ Question 2: Effective in identifying challenges but lacked depth. Explore probing questions for more detailed insights.

✓ Question 3: Open-ended and led to a fruitful discussion. Continue incorporating similar questions.

Action Plan: Set a goal to use at least two probing questions in the next team meeting to enhance the depth of discussions.

By actively utilizing these self-assessment tools, readers will gain a comprehensive understanding of their questioning techniques. The templates provided offer a structured approach to self-reflection, allowing individuals to systematically identify strengths, areas for improvement, and actionable strategies for refining their questioning skills in various professional contexts.

Importance & Benefits of Being a Good Listener

Listening is a foundational element of effective communication, often overlooked in the spotlight of questioning. This chapter explores the profound impact of active listening on relationships, productivity, and overall communication effectiveness. Through case studies and real-life examples, readers will gain a deep understanding of the importance and benefits of being a good listener.

Exploring the Impact on Relationships: Active listening is the bedrock of meaningful relationships, both personal and professional. By genuinely engaging with others through attentive listening, individuals foster trust, empathy, and understanding. This section delves into how being a good listener contributes to the cultivation of positive and healthy relationships.

Example – Personal Relationships: Consider a scenario where a friend is going through a challenging time. Instead of offering immediate solutions, an active listener might say, "I hear that you're going through a tough situation. How can I support you?" This empathetic approach not only strengthens the friendship but also provides the space for the friend to express their emotions.

Impact on Productivity: In the professional realm, being a good listener directly influences productivity. By understanding the needs, concerns, and ideas of team members, leaders can make informed decisions, foster innovation, and enhance overall team dynamics. This section explores how active listening contributes to a more productive and efficient work environment.

Case Study – Team Collaboration: A case study might highlight a team facing challenges in a project. The team leader, through active listening in team meetings, identifies the underlying issues and collaboratively works with team members to implement solutions. This not only resolves the challenges but also strengthens team cohesion and boosts productivity.

Benefits of Understanding Unspoken Cues: A significant aspect of being a good listener is the ability to comprehend non-verbal cues, such as body language and tone of voice. This skill provides valuable insights into the emotional state and intentions of the speaker. The benefits of deciphering unspoken cues are explored in this section.

Example – Negotiation: In a negotiation scenario, a skilled negotiator not only listens to the words spoken but also pays attention to the body language and tone of the other party. This nuanced listening allows the negotiator to gauge the sincerity of the counterparty and adjust their approach accordingly.

Action Plan for Enhancing Listening Skills: To encourage readers to actively develop their listening skills, an action plan will be provided. This may involve self-assessment of current listening habits, setting specific listening goals, and engaging in reflective exercises to strengthen this essential aspect of communication.

Real-life Scenario – Reflective Listening Practice: In a reflective listening exercise, readers might pair up and take turns discussing a topic while the listener practices paraphrasing and summarizing the speaker's points. This hands-on approach helps individuals recognize their listening strengths and areas for improvement.

By understanding the profound impact of active listening on relationships and productivity, readers will be motivated to prioritize and enhance their listening skills. The chapter serves as a bridge, connecting the art of questioning with the equally crucial skill of listening. As readers move forward, they will be equipped to holistically approach communication, creating a positive and impactful dynamic in both personal and professional spheres.

Importance & Benefits of Being a Good Listener-Enhancing Listening Skills Action Plan

This section emphasizes the significance and benefits of being a good listener. The action plan provided encourages readers to actively develop their listening skills through self-assessment, goal-setting, and reflective exercises. The templates and examples offered aim to guide individuals in systematically enhancing this crucial aspect of communication.

Enhancing Listening Skills Action Plan:

Self-Assessment of Current Listening Habits:

- ✓ *Objective:* Reflect on current listening habits and identify strengths and areas for improvement.
- ✓ *Template: List:* Identify common listening behaviors.
- ✓ *Rating:* Rate the effectiveness of each behavior.
- ✓ *Reflection: "I often interrupt others while they speak, hindering my ability to fully grasp their perspectives."*

Setting Specific Listening Goals:

- ✓ *Objective:* Establish clear and measurable goals for improving listening skills.
- ✓ *Template: Goal Setting:* Define specific listening goals (e.g., reducing interruptions, practicing active listening).
- ✓ *Timeline:* Set a realistic timeframe for achieving each goal.
- ✓ *Commitment Statement:* Declare commitment to enhancing listening skills.

Reflective Listening Journal:

- ✓ *Objective:* Maintain a journal for reflective listening practices.
- ✓ *Template: Entry:* Document key listening behaviors in recent interactions.
- ✓ *Reflection:* Analyze the effectiveness of listening habits and note areas for improvement.
- ✓ *Action Plan:* Set goals for refining listening techniques based on reflections.

Listening Skill Progress Tracker:

- ✓ *Objective:* Monitor progress in developing listening skills.
- ✓ *Template: Skills:* List specific listening skills to develop (e.g., paraphrasing, maintaining eye contact).
- ✓ *Progress Rating:* Regularly assess and rate progress in each skill.
- ✓ *Celebrating Achievements:* Acknowledge milestones and improvements.

Feedback from Others:

- ✓ *Objective:* Seek feedback on listening habits from peers or mentors.
- ✓ *Template: Request for Feedback:* Ask specific questions about listening behaviors.

- ✓ *Feedback Analysis:* Reflect on received feedback and identify actionable insights.
- ✓ *Improvement Plan:* Develop strategies based on feedback for continuous improvement.

Example Reflective Listening Journal Entry:

Date: [Date]

Interaction Summary: Team brainstorming session.

Listening Habits Observed:

- ✓ Interrupted team members while sharing ideas.
- ✓ Frequently checked phone during discussions.
- ✓ Struggled to paraphrase and summarize others' points effectively.

Reflection:

- ✓ Interruptions hindered the flow of ideas. Practice patience and let others finish before responding.
- ✓ Phone distractions indicated a lack of focus. Implement a 'no-phone' rule during team discussions.
- ✓ Ineffective paraphrasing demonstrated a need for active listening enhancement.

Action Plan: Set a goal for the next team meeting to avoid interruptions, stay focused, and practice effective paraphrasing.

By actively engaging in this action plan, readers will not only recognize the importance of effective listening but also develop actionable strategies to enhance their listening skills. The templates and examples provided offer practical insights into self-assessment, goal-setting, and reflective exercises, ensuring that readers systematically improve their listening capabilities in both personal and professional contexts.

Why We Don't Listen

Listening seems like a simple act, yet many factors can impede our ability to do it effectively. This chapter delves into the common barriers to effective listening, exploring both personal and environmental obstacles. By understanding why we often fall short in our listening endeavors, readers can develop strategies to overcome these challenges and become more attentive and engaged listeners.

Common Barriers to Effective Listening: Effective listening requires more than just the physical act of hearing. Various barriers can impede our ability to truly absorb and understand the messages being communicated. This section identifies and examines these barriers, which may include psychological, emotional, and environmental factors.

Example – Psychological Barrier: A psychological barrier to effective listening could be preoccupation with personal concerns. For instance, if someone is dealing with a stressful situation at home, they might find it challenging to fully concentrate during a work meeting, hindering their ability to listen attentively.

Example – Environmental Barrier: Environmental distractions, such as noisy surroundings or interruptions, can also create barriers to effective listening. In a classroom setting, for instance, external noise or disruptions can make it difficult for students to focus on the lecture.

Strategies to Overcome Personal Barriers: Personal barriers to effective listening often stem from internal factors such as preconceived notions, biases, or emotional states. This section provides strategies to help individuals recognize and overcome these barriers, fostering a mindset conducive to active listening.

Example – Overcoming Biases: If someone holds biases or judgments about a speaker, it can impede their ability to listen objectively. An individual may employ a strategy like mindfulness, consciously acknowledging and setting aside their biases before engaging in a conversation to ensure a more open-minded approach.

Strategies to Overcome Environmental Barriers: Environmental factors, such as noise or distractions, can significantly impact listening. This section offers practical strategies to create a conducive listening environment, whether at home, in the workplace, or other settings.

Example – Workplace Environment: In a noisy office, an individual might use noise-canceling headphones or find a quiet space for important phone calls or discussions. By taking proactive steps to control the environment, they enhance their ability to focus and listen effectively.

Action Plan for Improved Listening: To empower readers to enhance their listening skills, an action plan will be provided. This may involve self-reflection exercises, setting specific listening goals, and implementing strategies to overcome personal and environmental barriers.

Real-life Scenario – Reflective Listening Journal: Readers might be encouraged to maintain a reflective listening journal for a week. In this journal, they document instances where they faced challenges in listening and note the strategies they employed to overcome those challenges. This reflective practice helps reinforce positive listening habits.

By examining the reasons why we often struggle to listen effectively and providing actionable strategies to overcome these obstacles, this chapter equips readers with the tools to become more attentive listeners. As readers progress through the subsequent chapters, they will be able to apply these strategies in real-world scenarios, creating a positive shift in their communication dynamics.

Why We Don't Listen - Improved Listening Action Plan

This section explores common barriers to effective listening and provides an action plan to empower readers to enhance their listening skills. The action plan involves self-reflection exercises, goal-setting, and strategies to overcome both personal and environmental barriers. The examples and templates aim to guide individuals in systematically improving their listening capabilities.

Improved Listening Action Plan:

Self-Reflection on Listening Habits:
- ✓ *Objective:* Reflect on personal listening habits and identify patterns that hinder effective listening.
- ✓ *Template: Questionnaire:* Answer reflective questions about recent listening experiences.
- ✓ *Analysis:* Identify common barriers to effective listening.
- ✓ *Insights:* Gain insights into personal listening patterns.

Setting Specific Listening Goals:
- ✓ *Objective:* Establish clear and measurable goals for improving listening skills.

- ✓ *Template: Goal Setting:* Define specific listening goals (e.g., reducing distractions, practicing empathy).
- ✓ *Timeline:* Set a realistic timeframe for achieving each goal.
- ✓ *Commitment Statement:* Declare commitment to overcoming listening barriers.

Strategies to Overcome Personal Barriers:
- ✓ *Objective:* Develop strategies to address individual barriers to effective listening.
- ✓ *Template: Identify Barriers:* List personal barriers identified through self-reflection.
- ✓ *Strategies:* Outline actionable strategies to overcome each identified barrier.
- ✓ *Implementation Plan:* Detail how each strategy will be implemented in daily interactions.

Environment Optimization Checklist:
- ✓ *Objective:* Assess and optimize the listening environment for better focus.
- ✓ *Template: Checklist:* Identify environmental factors impacting listening (e.g., noise, distractions).
- ✓ *Adjustment Plan:* List specific adjustments to create an optimal listening environment.
- ✓ *Monitoring Progress:* Regularly evaluate the effectiveness of environmental adjustments.

Feedback and Accountability Partner:
- ✓ *Objective:* Seek feedback from peers or designate an accountability partner for mutual support.
- ✓ *Template: Feedback Request:* Ask for feedback on listening habits and potential improvements.
- ✓ *Accountability Agreement:* Establish a mutual commitment with an accountability partner.

- ✓ *Check-In Schedule:* Set regular check-ins to discuss progress and challenges.

Example Self-Reflection Questionnaire:

Questionnaire: Why We Don't Listen

- ✓ Do you find yourself interrupting others before they finish speaking?
- ✓ How often do external distractions (phone, surroundings) impact your ability to listen?
- ✓ Are you prone to forming judgments or assumptions before fully understanding the speaker's perspective?

Analysis:

- ✓ Frequent interruptions hinder effective listening.
- ✓ External distractions contribute to a lack of focus.
- ✓ Premature judgments indicate a need for improved empathy and understanding.

Insights:

- ✓ Patience needs improvement.
- ✓ Establishing a distraction-free environment is crucial.
- ✓ Practicing empathy is key to overcoming preconceived judgments.

By actively engaging in this action plan, readers will not only gain insights into their personal listening barriers but also develop actionable strategies to overcome them. The templates and examples provided offer practical insights into self-reflection, goal-setting, and strategies for overcoming both personal and environmental barriers to effective listening, fostering improved communication skills.

Types/Modes of Listening

Listening is a dynamic process that takes various forms depending on the context and the goals of the communication. This chapter explores different types or modes of listening, dissecting the nuances of active, passive, empathetic, and critical listening. By understanding when and how to apply each mode, readers can cultivate a more versatile and effective listening repertoire.

Active Listening: Active listening is a focused and intentional form of listening where the listener fully engages with the speaker. This mode involves not only hearing the words but also interpreting and responding to the message. It is particularly effective in situations where understanding and empathy are crucial.

Example – Active Listening in a Counseling Session: In a counseling session, the counselor might use active listening by paraphrasing the client's feelings and asking clarifying questions. This demonstrates genuine engagement and encourages the client to express themselves more openly.

Passive Listening: Passive listening involves hearing the words without necessarily responding or fully engaging with the speaker. While it may seem less involved, passive listening can be appropriate in certain contexts, such as when receiving information without the need for immediate feedback.

Example – Passive Listening in a Lecture: In a lecture setting, students may engage in passive listening to absorb information. The focus is on receiving the content, and interaction with the speaker is minimal.

Empathetic Listening: Empathetic listening goes beyond understanding the words spoken; it involves connecting with the speaker on an emotional level. This mode is particularly valuable in situations where emotional support and understanding are essential.

Example – Empathetic Listening in a Supportive Conversation: If a friend is sharing a personal challenge, empathetic listening involves not only understanding the details but also expressing genuine concern and compassion. Phrases like, "I can imagine that must be really tough for you" convey empathy.

Critical Listening: Critical listening involves analyzing and evaluating the content of the message. This mode is employed when it's essential to assess the accuracy, validity, or reliability of the information being presented.

Example – Critical Listening in a Business Presentation: In a business presentation, critical listening may involve evaluating the evidence, assessing the speaker's credibility, and questioning assumptions. This mode helps the listener make informed decisions based on the information presented.

When to Apply Each Mode: The effectiveness of listening depends on choosing the appropriate mode for the given situation. This section provides guidance on when to apply each listening mode based on the communication context.

Action Plan for Developing Listening Modes: Readers will be encouraged to reflect on their natural tendencies in different listening modes and identify areas for improvement. Through scenario-based exercises, they will practice switching between listening modes and develop an action plan for enhancing their versatility as listeners.

Real-life Scenario – Workplace Communication: Consider a workplace scenario where a manager needs to address an employee concern. The manager might start with empathetic listening to understand the employee's perspective, transition to active listening by asking clarifying questions, and finally engage in critical listening to assess potential solutions.

By exploring the different types or modes of listening and providing practical guidance on when to apply each, this chapter equips readers with a nuanced understanding of the listening process. As readers integrate these insights into their daily communication practices, they will become more adaptable and effective listeners in diverse situations. The subsequent chapters will further build on this foundation, offering a comprehensive approach to mastering the art of questioning and listening.

Types/Modes of Listening - Developing Listening Modes Action Plan

This section explores different types or modes of listening and aims to enhance readers' versatility as listeners. The action plan involves reflection on natural listening tendencies, scenario-based exercises to practice switching between modes, and the development of an action plan for improvement. The examples and templates provided offer practical guidance for readers to systematically enhance their listening versatility.

Developing Listening Modes Action Plan:
Reflection on Natural Listening Tendencies:

- ✓ *Objective:* Reflect on personal tendencies in different listening modes.
- ✓ *Template: Mode Identification:* Identify natural inclinations in modes like active, passive, empathetic, and critical listening.
- ✓ *Analysis:* Assess the effectiveness of each mode in various scenarios.
- ✓ *Reflection:* Recognize areas where improvement is needed.

Scenario-Based Exercises for Mode Switching:

- ✓ *Objective:* Practice switching between different listening modes in scenario-based exercises.
- ✓ *Template: Scenarios:* Develop scenarios representing diverse listening situations (e.g., counseling session, team meeting, social gathering).
- ✓ *Mode Identification:* Assign specific listening modes to each scenario.
- ✓ *Reflection and Analysis:* After each exercise, reflect on the effectiveness of mode switching and identify challenges.

Action Plan for Versatility Enhancement:

- ✓ *Objective:* Develop a personalized action plan for enhancing versatility in listening modes.
- ✓ *Template: Identify Goals:* Define specific goals for improvement in each listening mode.
- ✓ *Strategies:* Outline strategies to practice and reinforce each mode.
- ✓ *Timeline:* Set a realistic timeline for achieving enhanced versatility.
- ✓ *Progress Tracking:* Create a system for monitoring progress and adjustments.

Peer Feedback and Collaboration:

- ✓ *Objective:* Seek feedback from peers on listening modes and collaborate to improve collectively.
- ✓ *Template: Feedback Exchange:* Engage in mutual feedback on listening behaviors.
- ✓ *Collaborative Goals:* Establish shared goals for enhancing listening modes.
- ✓ *Regular Check-Ins:* Schedule regular check-ins to discuss progress and challenges.

Example Reflection on Natural Listening Tendencies:

Active Listening:

- ✓ Natural Inclination: Actively engages in discussions, asks clarifying questions.
- ✓ Effectiveness: Facilitates understanding but may sometimes come across as overly assertive.

Empathetic Listening:

- ✓ Natural Inclination: Expresses understanding and empathy, but struggles to maintain objectivity.
- ✓ Effectiveness: Builds strong connections, but may need to balance emotional involvement.

Example Scenario-Based Exercise:

Scenario: Team Meeting

- ✓ *Listening Mode Assignment:* Practice active listening during a team brainstorming session.
- ✓ *Reflection and Analysis:* After the exercise, analyze how well active listening was applied, and identify areas for improvement, such as allowing more space for others to contribute.

By actively engaging in this action plan, readers will gain a deeper understanding of their natural tendencies in different listening modes and develop strategies for enhancing their versatility. The templates and examples provided offer practical insights into self-reflection, scenario-based exercises, and personalized action planning, fostering improved listening capabilities in diverse situations.

Barriers to Effective Listening

Effective listening is not always a straightforward process; numerous barriers, both internal and external, can hinder our ability to fully engage with and comprehend the messages being communicated. This chapter delves into these barriers, exploring the psychological, emotional, and environmental factors that impede effective listening. By understanding these barriers and implementing solutions, readers can enhance their capacity to be attentive and engaged listeners.

Internal Barriers to Effective Listening:

Preconceived Notions and Biases: Pre-existing beliefs or biases can cloud our ability to objectively receive information. For instance, if someone holds a strong opinion about a certain topic, they may selectively listen to information that aligns with their views.

Solution: The key is to cultivate awareness of one's biases and actively work towards setting them aside during communication. Reflective practices and self-awareness exercises can aid in identifying and addressing these internal barriers.

Personal Stress and Distractions: Internal stressors, such as personal issues or a busy mind, can divert attention away from the speaker. This may result in a lack of focus and comprehension.

Solution: Developing mindfulness techniques, such as deep breathing or meditation, can help manage personal stress and enhance mental clarity. Creating a conducive listening environment by minimizing distractions is also crucial.

Example – Overcoming Distractions: Imagine a student trying to study in a noisy environment. By recognizing the distraction and moving to a quieter space, the student can overcome the internal barrier of environmental noise, enabling more effective listening to study materials.

External Barriers to Effective Listening:

Environmental Distractions: External factors such as noise, interruptions, or uncomfortable seating arrangements can significantly impact listening. In a crowded or noisy environment, it may be challenging to focus on the speaker's message.

Solution: Proactively managing the environment by finding a quieter space or using noise-canceling tools can mitigate external distractions and improve listening conditions.

Poor Communication Channels: Ineffective communication channels, such as unclear audio, can hinder comprehension. This barrier is particularly relevant in virtual or remote communication where technical issues may arise.

Solution: Ensuring the use of reliable communication tools and addressing technical issues promptly contributes to overcoming external barriers related to communication channels.

Example – Virtual Meeting Enhancement: In a virtual meeting with poor audio quality, participants might struggle to understand each other. Addressing this barrier involves troubleshooting technical issues, using clear communication tools, and seeking feedback to ensure effective virtual communication.

Action Plan for Overcoming Barriers: Readers will engage in exercises to identify their own internal and external listening barriers. Through reflective practices, they will assess their common challenges and develop a personalized action plan to overcome these barriers systematically.

Real-life Scenario – Workplace Communication Enhancement: Consider a workplace scenario where a team faces communication challenges due to a noisy office environment. The team might collaboratively identify strategies to minimize noise, such as implementing designated quiet zones or using noise-canceling devices, thus overcoming external barriers to effective listening.

By thoroughly examining both internal and external barriers to effective listening and providing actionable solutions, this chapter equips readers with the tools to navigate challenges in their listening journey. As readers integrate these strategies into their daily communication practices, they will enhance their ability to overcome barriers, fostering a more attentive and engaged approach to listening. The subsequent chapters will build on this foundation, offering further insights into effective questioning and listening skills.

Barriers to Effective Listening - Overcoming Barriers Action Plan

This section explores the internal and external barriers to effective listening and provides an action plan for readers to systematically overcome these barriers. The action plan involves engaging in exercises to identify personal barriers, reflective practices, and the development of a personalized plan for improvement. The examples and templates provided offer practical guidance for readers to enhance their listening skills by addressing common challenges.

Overcoming Barriers Action Plan:
Identification of Internal Listening Barriers:
- ✓ *Objective:* Identify personal internal barriers to effective listening.
- ✓ *Template: Reflective Questions:* Answer questions that prompt self-reflection on internal barriers.
- ✓ *Barrier Analysis:* Assess how internal factors like preconceptions, emotions, or distractions impact listening.
- ✓ *Personal Insights:* Identify common challenges hindering effective listening.

Identification of External Listening Barriers:
- ✓ *Objective:* Identify external factors that serve as barriers to effective listening.
- ✓ *Template: Environmental Analysis:* Evaluate the impact of external factors (e.g., noise, interruptions) on listening.
- ✓ *Identifying Distractions:* List common external distractions that affect listening.
- ✓ *Barrier Categorization:* Classify external barriers into categories for clarity.

Reflective Practices for Common Challenges:
- ✓ *Objective:* Reflect on common challenges identified and their impact on listening.
- ✓ *Template: Challenge Analysis:* Break down each identified challenge into specific aspects.
- ✓ *Reflection on Impact:* Analyze how these challenges affect the quality of listening.
- ✓ *Learning from Challenges:* Extract lessons from each challenge for future improvement.

Personalized Action Plan for Improvement:
- ✓ *Objective:* Develop a personalized plan to systematically overcome identified barriers.

- ✓ *Template: Goal Setting:* Define specific goals for improvement related to internal and external barriers.
- ✓ *Strategies:* Outline actionable strategies to address each identified barrier.
- ✓ *Timeline:* Set a realistic timeline for achieving enhanced listening skills.
- ✓ *Monitoring Progress:* Create a system for monitoring progress and adjustments.

Example Identification of Internal Listening Barriers:

Internal Barrier: Preconceptions

- ✓ Reflection: *"I often enter conversations with preconceived notions about the speaker's perspective, limiting my ability to truly listen."*

Example Identification of External Listening Barriers:

External Barrier: Noisy Environment

- ✓ Categorization: Environmental Distractions
- ✓ Impact: *"Noise in my surroundings often hinders my ability to focus on the speaker's message."*

Example Reflective Practices for Common Challenges:

Common Challenge: Multitasking

- ✓ Challenge Analysis: Identify specific situations where multitasking hinders listening.
- ✓ Reflection on Impact: *"While multitasking, I miss crucial details in conversations, affecting the depth of my understanding."*

By actively engaging in this action plan, readers will not only identify their internal and external listening barriers but also develop actionable strategies for overcoming these challenges systematically. The templates and examples provided offer practical insights into self-reflection, barrier identification, and personalized action planning, fostering improved listening capabilities by addressing both internal and external obstacles.

Degrees/Levels of Active Listening

Active listening is not a one-size-fits-all skill; it exists along a continuum with varying degrees or levels. This chapter explores the hierarchy of active listening skills, guiding readers from foundational listening to advanced, nuanced forms of engagement. By understanding and developing these degrees of active listening, readers can refine their abilities to connect with others on a deeper level and extract richer meaning from communication.

Basic Listening Skills:
- ✓ **Attentive Listening:** At the foundational level, attentive listening involves giving one's full attention to the speaker. This includes maintaining eye contact, avoiding distractions, and nodding or providing other non-verbal cues to signal engagement.
- ✓ *Example:* Imagine a student actively listening to a teacher during a lecture, maintaining eye contact, and showing visible signs of attentiveness.
- ✓ **Paraphrasing:** Paraphrasing is the ability to restate or summarize the speaker's message in one's own words. It demonstrates comprehension and allows for clarification.
- ✓ *Example:* In a conversation, a listener might say, *"If I understand correctly, you're saying that..."*

Intermediate Listening Skills:
- ✓ **Reflective Listening:** Reflective listening involves echoing or mirroring the speaker's emotions or sentiments. It goes beyond the

content of the message to capture the underlying feelings.

✓ *Example:* If a friend expresses frustration about a situation, a reflective listener might respond with, "It sounds like you're really frustrated with how things are going."

✓ **Asking Clarifying Questions:** Intermediate listening includes the ability to ask questions that seek clarification or more information. This demonstrates an active effort to fully understand the speaker's perspective.

✓ *Example:* In a work meeting, a team member might ask, *"Could you elaborate a bit more on the specific challenges you've encountered in this project?"*

Advanced Listening Skills:

✓ **Empathetic Listening:** Empathetic listening involves not only understanding the speaker's emotions but also connecting with and validating those emotions. It requires a deep level of emotional intelligence.

✓ *Example:* If a colleague shares a personal struggle, an empathetic listener might respond with, *"I can imagine that this situation is really tough for you. How can I support you?"*

✓ **Analytical Listening:** At the advanced level, analytical listening involves critically evaluating the information presented. It includes assessing the speaker's credibility, identifying biases, and evaluating the overall validity of the message.

✓ *Example:* In a business negotiation, an analytically listening professional might critically assess the evidence and arguments presented by the other party, seeking to understand the negotiation dynamics more deeply.

Developing an Action Plan: Readers will engage in a reflective exercise to assess their current active listening skills and identify areas for improvement. Based on this self-assessment, they will create a personalized action plan that targets specific degrees or levels of active listening for development.

Real-life Scenario – Personal Growth Conversations: Consider a scenario where friends engage in a conversation about personal growth. The participants progress through various levels of active listening, starting with attentive listening, moving to reflective listening about emotional challenges, and eventually engaging in empathetic listening to support each other's growth journeys.

By mapping out the degrees or levels of active listening and providing examples at each stage, this chapter equips readers with a comprehensive framework for developing and refining their listening skills. As readers progress through the subsequent chapters, they will be able to apply this understanding in diverse contexts, fostering more profound and meaningful connections through active listening.

Degrees/Levels of Active Listening - Developing an Action Plan

This section delves into the various degrees or levels of active listening and guides readers in developing an action plan to enhance their active listening skills. The action plan involves a reflective exercise to assess current active listening skills, identify areas for improvement, and create a personalized plan targeting specific degrees or levels of active listening. The examples and templates provided aim to assist readers in systematically elevating their active listening capabilities.

Developing an Action Plan:

Reflective Exercise for Self-Assessment:

- ✓ *Objective:* Reflect on current active listening skills and identify strengths and areas for improvement.
- ✓ *Template: Self-Assessment Questions:* Pose questions that prompt reflection on different aspects of active listening.
- ✓ *Strengths Identification:* Recognize personal strengths in active listening.
- ✓ *Areas for Improvement:* Identify specific aspects that need enhancement.

Identification of Degrees/Levels of Active Listening:

- ✓ *Objective:* Understand the various degrees or levels of active listening.
- ✓ *Template: Degrees Identification:* Define different levels of active listening (e.g., basic, advanced, empathetic).
- ✓ *Characteristics:* Outline the characteristics associated with each level.
- ✓ *Personal Connection:* Relate personal experiences to each degree for better comprehension.

Creation of a Personalized Action Plan:

- ✓ *Objective:* Develop a targeted plan for improving active listening skills based on self-assessment.
- ✓ *Template: Goal Setting:* Define specific goals for improvement in active listening degrees.
- ✓ *Strategies:* Outline actionable strategies to enhance active listening at each level.

- ✓ *Timeline:* Set a realistic timeline for achieving improvements.
- ✓ *Monitoring Progress:* Establish mechanisms for monitoring progress and making adjustments.

Example Reflective Exercise for Self-Assessment:

- ✓ *Self-Assessment Question: "How often do I paraphrase or summarize the speaker's message to confirm understanding during conversations?"*
- ✓ *Reflection: "I realize that I rarely use paraphrasing in conversations, potentially missing opportunities to ensure accurate understanding."*

Example Identification of Degrees/Levels of Active Listening:

Degree: Basic Active Listening

- ✓ Characteristics: Demonstrating non-verbal cues, providing occasional feedback.
- ✓ Personal Connection: *"During team meetings, I often nod in agreement, but I can improve by occasionally summarizing key points to show active engagement."*

Example Personalized Action Plan:

Goal: Enhance Basic Active Listening

- ✓ Strategies: Practice paraphrasing during team discussions.
- ✓ Timeline: Implement in the next three team meetings.
- ✓ Monitoring Progress: Solicit feedback from team members on the effectiveness of paraphrasing.

By actively engaging in this action plan, readers will gain a comprehensive understanding of their active listening skills, identify specific degrees or levels for improvement, and create a personalized plan for enhancement. The templates and examples provided offer practical insights into self-assessment, degree identification, and targeted goal-setting, fostering a systematic improvement in active listening capabilities.

The Process of Listening

Listening is a dynamic and multifaceted process that goes beyond merely hearing words. This chapter dissects the stages of effective listening, guiding readers through the journey of receiving, interpreting, and responding to messages. By breaking down the intricate process of listening, readers can gain a deeper understanding of how to engage with information in a meaningful and intentional manner.

Stage 1: Receiving the Message:
- ✓ **Physical Reception:** The initial stage involves the reception of auditory stimuli. It requires the physical act of hearing, where sound waves are processed by the ears and transmitted to the brain.
- ✓ **Selective Attention:** Selective attention entails focusing on specific stimuli while filtering out others. It is the cognitive process of prioritizing relevant information, allowing for a more targeted reception of the message.
- ✓ *Example:* In a crowded café, a person selectively attends to their friend's voice, filtering out background noise to concentrate on the conversation.

Stage 2: Interpreting the Message:
- ✓ **Comprehension:** Comprehension involves making sense of the received information. It includes understanding the meaning of words, phrases, and the overall context in which the message is delivered.
- ✓ *Example:* When reading a complex article, comprehension involves not only recognizing individual words but also understanding the

relationships between them to grasp the intended meaning.
- ✓ **Interpretation and Analysis:** Beyond comprehension, this stage involves interpreting the deeper meaning of the message. It requires analytical thinking to extract nuances, identify key points, and recognize underlying emotions.
- ✓ *Example:* In a business meeting, interpreting a colleague's proposal involves not only understanding the surface-level content but also analyzing the implications and potential outcomes.

Stage 3: Responding to the Message:
- ✓ **Verbal and Non-verbal Feedback:** Responding to a message involves providing feedback, either verbally or non-verbally. Verbal feedback may include asking questions or expressing agreement, while non-verbal cues such as nodding or facial expressions convey engagement.
- ✓ *Example:* During a conversation, a listener may offer verbal feedback by saying, "I see your perspective," and non-verbal feedback by nodding in agreement.
- ✓ **Confirmation and Clarification:** Confirming understanding or seeking clarification is an essential component of effective listening. It ensures that the listener accurately grasps the speaker's intended message.
- ✓ *Example:* If there is ambiguity in a colleague's instructions, seeking clarification might involve saying, *"Just to confirm, are you asking for A or B in this report?"*

Exercises to Enhance Listening Capabilities:

- ✓ **Reflective Listening Exercise:** Readers engage in a reflective listening exercise where they listen to a short audio clip or engage in a conversation and subsequently reflect on their comprehension and interpretation of the message.
- ✓ **Selective Attention Challenge:** A practical exercise challenges readers to focus on specific auditory stimuli while disregarding competing sounds, simulating the cognitive aspect of selective attention.
- ✓ **Feedback Role-play:** Through role-playing scenarios, readers practice providing both verbal and non-verbal feedback in various communication contexts, enhancing their responsiveness as listeners.

Action Plan for Continuous Improvement: Readers develop an action plan based on their self-assessment of the listening process. This involves setting goals for improvement in specific stages of the listening journey, incorporating feedback mechanisms, and regularly practicing the identified exercises.

Real-life Scenario – Team Workshop: Imagine a team workshop where members engage in a listening exercise involving a presentation. Afterward, team members share their interpretations, provide feedback, and collectively discuss how they can enhance their listening skills in future collaborative endeavors.

By breaking down the process of listening into distinct stages and providing practical exercises, this chapter empowers readers to navigate each phase with intentionality. As readers apply these insights to real-life scenarios and commit to continuous improvement, they will cultivate a heightened awareness of the intricate process of listening, leading to more effective and meaningful interactions in both personal and professional settings.

The Process of Listening - Continuous Improvement Action Plan

This section explores the stages of the listening process and guides readers in developing an action plan for continuous improvement. The action plan involves self-assessment of the listening process, goal-setting for improvement in specific stages, feedback mechanisms, and regular practice of identified exercises. The examples and templates provided aim to assist readers in systematically enhancing their overall listening capabilities.

Continuous Improvement Action Plan:

Self-Assessment of the Listening Process:

- ✓ *Objective:* Reflect on personal listening habits and identify strengths and areas for improvement at different stages of the listening process.
- ✓ *Template: Listening Process Breakdown:* Identify stages such as receiving, interpreting, evaluating, and responding.
- ✓ *Self-Reflection Questions:* Pose questions that prompt consideration of behaviors at each stage.
- ✓ *Strengths and Weaknesses:* Identify specific strengths and weaknesses in the listening process.

Goal-Setting for Improvement:

- ✓ *Objective:* Establish clear goals for improvement in each stage of the listening process.

- ✓ *Template: Stage-Specific Goals:* Define specific, measurable goals for receiving, interpreting, evaluating, and responding.
- ✓ *Strategies:* Outline strategies for achieving improvement in each identified stage.
- ✓ *Timeline:* Set a realistic timeline for achieving goals.

Feedback Mechanisms:
- ✓ *Objective:* Develop mechanisms for obtaining feedback on listening behaviors at different process stages.
- ✓ *Template: Feedback Request Form:* Create a form for soliciting feedback from peers or mentors.
- ✓ *Frequency of Feedback:* Define a schedule for regular feedback sessions.
- ✓ *Actionable Feedback:* Specify the type of feedback desired for each listening stage.

Regular Practice and Exercises:
- ✓ *Objective:* Incorporate regular practice of exercises designed to improve specific stages of the listening process.
- ✓ *Template: Exercise Selection:* Identify exercises targeting each stage of the listening process.
- ✓ *Frequency of Practice:* Establish a practice schedule for regular incorporation of exercises.
- ✓ *Reflection on Exercises:* Develop a reflection template for assessing the effectiveness of each exercise.

Example Self-Assessment of the Listening Process:

Stage: Interpreting

- ✓ *Self-Reflection Question: "How often do I ask clarifying questions to ensure accurate understanding during conversations?"*
- ✓ *Analysis: "I realize that I rarely ask clarifying questions, leading to potential misunderstandings."*

Example Goal-Setting for Improvement:

Stage: Evaluating

- ✓ *Goal:* "Increase my ability to provide constructive feedback by actively summarizing and reflecting on others' viewpoints during team discussions."
- ✓ *Strategies:* Practice summarizing key points during team meetings, seek feedback on the effectiveness of evaluations.
- ✓ *Timeline:* Implement strategies in the next four team discussions.

Example Feedback Mechanisms:

Feedback Request Form:

- ✓ *Stage: Responding*
- ✓ *Specific Request:* "Please provide feedback on the clarity and effectiveness of my responses during our project update meetings."

Example Regular Practice and Exercises:

Exercise Selection:

- ✓ *Stage: Receiving*
- ✓ *Exercise:* Mindful listening exercise – focus on eliminating distractions and fully concentrating during a conversation.
- ✓ *Reflection on Exercise:* "This exercise helped me realize the impact of distractions on my receiving stage and motivated me to create a dedicated listening space."

By actively engaging in this action plan, readers will not only understand their listening process but also develop actionable strategies for improvement at each stage. The templates and examples provided offer practical insights into self-assessment, goal-setting, feedback mechanisms, and regular practice, fostering continuous enhancement in the overall listening journey.

Steps to Be an Effective Listener

Becoming an effective listener is a journey that requires intentional effort and continuous improvement. This chapter lays out practical steps to enhance listening skills, guiding readers through actionable strategies to implement active listening in their daily interactions. By embracing these steps, readers can transform their approach to communication, fostering deeper connections and understanding.

Step 1: Cultivate the Right Mindset: Effective listening begins with the right mindset. This involves approaching conversations with an open mind, a genuine curiosity to understand others, and a willingness to set aside personal biases.

Example: A professional entering a team meeting with a mindset focused on collaboration and understanding, rather than preconceived notions, creates an environment conducive to effective listening.

Step 2: Remove Distractions: Creating a conducive listening environment requires minimizing distractions. This involves putting away electronic devices, finding a quiet space, and ensuring that both the listener and speaker can fully engage without external interruptions.

Example: In a workplace setting, turning off email notifications and finding a quiet meeting room can help remove distractions and create a focused listening environment.

Step 3: Practice Active Presence: Being an effective listener involves more than just hearing; it requires active presence. This means maintaining eye contact, nodding to signal engagement, and using positive body language to convey interest.

Example: In a personal conversation, maintaining eye contact and nodding affirmatively signals to the speaker that their words are being actively received and understood.

Step 4: Ask Open-ended Questions: Encouraging meaningful dialogue involves asking open-ended questions that invite the speaker to share more detailed information. This promotes a deeper understanding of the speaker's perspective.

Example: Instead of asking a closed-ended question like, "Did you enjoy the presentation?" an effective listener might ask, "What aspects of the presentation resonated with you the most?"

Step 5: Paraphrase and Summarize: Demonstrating comprehension involves paraphrasing and summarizing the speaker's message. This not only confirms understanding but also provides an opportunity for the speaker to clarify or expand on their points.

Example: After a colleague explains a project proposal, an effective listener might say, "If I understand correctly, the key goals of the project are X, Y, and Z. Is that accurate?"

Step 6: Practice Empathetic Listening: Empathy is a cornerstone of effective listening. This step involves not only understanding the speaker's words but also connecting with their emotions and expressing genuine empathy.

Example: If a friend shares a difficult experience, an empathetic listener might respond with, "I can imagine that this situation is really tough for you. How can I support you?"

Step 7: Minimize Interrupting: Allowing the speaker to express their thoughts without interruption is crucial for effective listening. Minimizing interruptions demonstrates respect for the speaker's perspective and fosters a more open and collaborative dialogue.

Example: In a team brainstorming session, an effective listener refrains from interrupting colleagues, allowing each person to contribute their ideas without disruption.

Step 8: Provide Constructive Feedback: Effective listeners go beyond passive reception; they provide constructive feedback that encourages further conversation. This involves offering insights, asking follow-up questions, and contributing to the dialogue.

Example: After a team member presents a project update, an effective listener might provide constructive feedback by saying, "I appreciate the thoroughness of your analysis. Have you considered incorporating XYZ into the next phase?"

Action Plan for Continuous Improvement: Readers will develop a personalized action plan based on these steps. This involves self-assessment, setting specific goals for improvement in listening skills, and incorporating these steps into daily interactions.

Real-life Scenario – Family Dinner Conversation: Imagine a family dinner where members actively implement these steps. They cultivate a positive mindset, remove distractions, practice active presence, and engage in open-ended questions, creating an environment of effective listening that enhances family communication.

By following these practical steps and incorporating active listening into daily interactions, readers can transform their communication habits. The chapter serves as a guide for readers to cultivate the habits of effective listening, ultimately leading to more meaningful and productive conversations in various aspects of their lives. As readers continue on their journey of improvement, they will witness the positive impact of these steps on their relationships and overall communication effectiveness.

Steps to Be an Effective Listener - Continuous Improvement Action Plan

This section outlines the steps to be an effective listener and guides readers in developing a personalized action plan for continuous improvement. The action plan involves self-assessment, goal-setting for improvement in listening skills, and the incorporation of these steps into daily interactions. The examples and templates provided aim to assist readers in systematically enhancing their overall listening capabilities.

Continuous Improvement Action Plan:

Self-Assessment of Current Listening Skills:
- ✓ *Objective:* Reflect on current listening skills and identify strengths and areas for improvement.
- ✓ *Template: Self-Assessment Checklist:* Create a checklist with statements on various listening skills.
- ✓ *Scoring System:* Develop a scoring system to quantify the level of proficiency in each skill.
- ✓ *Areas for Improvement:* Identify specific skills that need enhancement.

Setting Specific Goals for Improvement:
- ✓ *Objective:* Establish clear, measurable goals for improvement in listening skills.

- ✓ *Template: Skill-Specific Goals:* Define goals for active listening, paraphrasing, empathy, and other key skills.
- ✓ *Strategies:* Outline actionable strategies for achieving improvement in each identified skill.
- ✓ *Timeline:* Set a realistic timeline for achieving goals.

Incorporating Steps into Daily Interactions:

- ✓ *Objective:* Integrate the identified steps into daily communication to reinforce positive listening habits.
- ✓ *Template: Daily Interaction Plan:* Create a plan outlining how to incorporate each step into different interactions.
- ✓ *Reflections:* Develop a reflection template to assess the effectiveness of applying steps.
- ✓ *Adjustment Strategies:* Include strategies for making real-time adjustments based on reflections.

Example Self-Assessment of Current Listening Skills:

Listening Skill: Empathy

- ✓ *Statement: "I make an effort to understand the emotions and perspectives of others during conversations."*
- ✓ *Scoring:* On a scale of 1-5, rate the level of effort in practicing empathy.
- ✓ *Analysis: "I scored a 3, indicating a moderate level of effort, but there is room for improvement in actively expressing empathy."*

Example Setting Specific Goals for Improvement:

Skill: Paraphrasing

- ✓ *Goal: "Enhance paraphrasing skills to confirm understanding and demonstrate active listening."*

- ✓ *Strategies:* Practice paraphrasing in various contexts, seek feedback on effectiveness.
- ✓ *Timeline:* Achieve a noticeable improvement within the next month.

Example Incorporating Steps into Daily Interactions:

Step: Give Full Attention

- ✓ *Daily Interaction Plan:* "During team meetings, I will eliminate distractions, put away electronic devices, and maintain eye contact to demonstrate full attention."
- ✓ *Reflections:* After each meeting, reflect on the effectiveness of giving full attention and note areas for improvement.
- ✓ *Adjustment Strategies:* If distractions persist, adjust the meeting environment or communication habits accordingly.

By actively engaging in this action plan, readers will not only understand the steps to be an effective listener but also develop actionable strategies for improvement. The templates and examples provided offer practical insights into self-assessment, goal-setting, and the integration of these steps into daily interactions, fostering continuous enhancement in overall listening skills.

Encouraging & Prompting Conversations

Effective communication is a two-way street, and fostering meaningful dialogue is essential for building strong connections. This chapter explores techniques to encourage and prompt conversations, creating an environment conducive to open communication. By mastering these techniques, readers can elevate their conversational skills, strengthen relationships, and promote a culture of openness and collaboration.

Creating a Positive Environment:

- ✓ **Build Trust:** Trust is the foundation of open communication. Establishing trust involves being reliable, transparent, and demonstrating integrity in all interactions.
- ✓ *Example:* A team leader consistently follows through on commitments and openly communicates about challenges, fostering trust within the team.
- ✓ **Demonstrate Empathy:** Creating a culture of open communication requires empathy. Acknowledge others' perspectives, validate their feelings, and show a genuine interest in understanding their experiences.
- ✓ *Example:* In a one-on-one conversation, expressing empathy might involve saying, *"I can see that this situation is challenging for you. How can we work together to find a solution?"*

Techniques to Encourage Meaningful Dialogue:

- ✓ **Active Listening Redux:** Active listening isn't just a step; it's an ongoing practice.

Continuously refining active listening skills involves consistently using techniques such as paraphrasing, summarizing, and providing constructive feedback.

- ✓ *Example:* In a team discussion, an effective communicator actively listens by paraphrasing a colleague's suggestion and adding, *"So, if I understand correctly, you're proposing..."*
- ✓ **Ask Open-ended Questions Strategically:** Open-ended questions prompt thoughtful responses and encourage deeper exploration of topics. Strategic use of open-ended questions guides conversations toward meaningful insights.
- ✓ *Example:* During a project review, a team member might ask, *"What challenges did you encounter during the implementation, and how can we address them moving forward?"*

Promoting Inclusivity:

- ✓ **Create a Safe Space for Expression:** Encouraging open communication requires creating a safe space where individuals feel comfortable expressing their thoughts, opinions, and concerns without fear of judgment.
- ✓ *Example:* A manager fosters a safe space by assuring team members that all perspectives are valued, and any concerns raised will be addressed constructively.
- ✓ **Diverse Perspectives Encouragement:** Actively seek out and welcome diverse perspectives. Encouraging individuals to share their unique viewpoints enriches discussions and promotes a culture of inclusivity.

- ✓ *Example:* In a brainstorming session, a team leader actively encourages participants to share diverse perspectives, emphasizing the importance of considering various angles.

Action Plan for Encouraging Conversations:
Readers will develop a personalized action plan for encouraging and prompting conversations. This involves reflecting on their current communication environment, setting specific goals for improvement, and incorporating the identified techniques into their daily interactions.

Real-life Scenario – Team Collaboration Session:
Imagine a team collaboration session where these techniques are implemented. The team leader sets a positive tone, actively listens to diverse perspectives, strategically uses open-ended questions, and creates a safe space for team members to express their ideas freely. This scenario showcases how these techniques contribute to a dynamic and productive team environment.

By mastering the techniques to encourage and prompt conversations, readers can transform their communication dynamics. This chapter serves as a guide for creating an environment where open communication flourishes, leading to more collaborative, innovative, and harmonious interactions. As readers apply these techniques in their personal and professional lives, they will contribute to the development of a positive communication culture within their communities and organizations.

Encouraging & Prompting Conversations - Action Plan

This section explores strategies for encouraging and prompting conversations and guides readers in developing a personalized action plan for improvement. The action plan involves reflecting on the current communication environment, setting specific goals, and incorporating identified techniques into daily interactions. The examples and templates provided aim to assist readers in fostering more open and meaningful communication.

Action Plan for Encouraging Conversations:

Reflecting on the Current Communication Environment:

- ✓ *Objective:* Assess the current state of communication in various settings.
- ✓ *Template: Communication Environment Analysis:* Identify strengths and weaknesses in the current communication environment.
- ✓ *Feedback Gathering:* Seek input from peers or colleagues on their perceptions of the communication atmosphere.
- ✓ *Identifying Opportunities:* Recognize areas for improvement and potential barriers.

Setting Specific Goals for Improvement:

- ✓ *Objective:* Establish clear and achievable goals for encouraging and prompting conversations.
- ✓ *Template: Goal Definition:* Define specific goals, such as increasing participation in meetings or fostering more open discussions.
- ✓ *Strategies:* Outline actionable strategies to achieve each identified goal.
- ✓ *Timeline:* Set a realistic timeline for achieving improvements.

Incorporating Identified Techniques into Daily Interactions:

- ✓ *Objective:* Integrate the identified techniques into daily communication to create a more conducive environment for conversation.
- ✓ *Template: Technique Integration Plan:* Develop a plan outlining how to incorporate techniques like active listening, open-ended questions, and affirmations.
- ✓ *Reflections:* Create a reflection template to assess the effectiveness of applying techniques.
- ✓ *Adjustment Strategies:* Include strategies for making real-time adjustments based on reflections.

Example Reflecting on the Current Communication Environment:

Strength: Collaborative Decision-Making

- ✓ *Analysis: "Our team excels in collaborative decision-making during formal meetings, but there's room for improvement in encouraging spontaneous conversations and idea-sharing."*

Example Setting Specific Goals for Improvement:

Goal: Increase Spontaneous Idea-Sharing

- ✓ *Strategies:* Encourage team members to share ideas during casual conversations, dedicate time for informal brainstorming sessions.
- ✓ *Timeline:* Noticeable improvement within the next two months.

Example Incorporating Identified Techniques into Daily Interactions:

Technique: Open-Ended Questions

- ✓ *Technique Integration Plan: "During team meetings, I will incorporate open-ended questions to stimulate deeper discussions and*

encourage team members to share their insights."
- ✓ *Reflections:* After each meeting, assess the impact of open-ended questions on the quality and depth of discussions.
- ✓ *Adjustment Strategies:* If responses are limited, adjust question framing or experiment with different techniques.

By actively engaging in this action plan, readers will not only understand techniques for encouraging and prompting conversations but also develop actionable strategies for improvement. The templates and examples provided offer practical insights into reflecting on the current communication environment, goal-setting, and the integration of identified techniques, fostering a more dynamic and inclusive communication atmosphere.

Action Plans and Exercises

Learning effective questioning and listening skills is not just about theory; it's about practical application and continuous improvement. This chapter focuses on hands-on activities and action plans designed to reinforce the concepts explored in the book. By engaging in these exercises and developing personalized action plans, readers can actively apply the skills they've learned and steadily enhance their communication abilities.

Hands-on Activities to Reinforce Concepts:

- ✓ **Scenario-based Role Play:** Engage in scenario-based role-play exercises where readers can practice effective questioning and listening skills in simulated real-life situations. This could include workplace scenarios, social interactions, or familial discussions.

  Example: In a workplace role-play, a reader may take on the role of a manager addressing an employee concern, actively applying the questioning and listening techniques learned.

- ✓ **Reflective Journaling:** Encourage readers to keep a reflective journal where they document their daily communication experiences. This includes instances where they successfully applied new skills and areas where they faced challenges. Reflection enhances self-awareness and facilitates continuous improvement.

  Example: A reflective journal entry might detail a conversation where a reader successfully used open-ended questions to navigate a challenging discussion.

- ✓ **Group Discussion and Feedback Sessions:** Form discussion groups where readers can share their experiences, discuss challenges, and provide constructive feedback to each other. This collaborative approach allows for collective learning and diverse perspectives.

  Example: In a group discussion, participants might share examples of effective questioning and listening in various contexts, providing insights that others can learn from.

Action Plans for Continuous Improvement:

- ✓ **Self-assessment Surveys:** Develop self-assessment surveys that allow readers to evaluate their questioning and listening skills. These surveys could cover different aspects, such as clarity of questions, depth of listening, and responsiveness.

  Example: A self-assessment question might ask, *"On a scale of 1 to 10, how effectively do you feel you listen to others during team meetings?"*

- ✓ **Goal-setting Exercises:** Guide readers in setting specific, measurable, achievable, relevant, and time-bound (SMART) goals for their questioning and listening skills. These goals can be short-term and long-term, focusing on specific aspects identified in the self-assessment.

  Example: A reader might set a SMART goal such as, *"Within the next month, I will practice asking at least three open-ended questions in each team meeting to enhance my questioning skills."*

- ✓ **Progress Tracking Tools:** Provide tools for readers to track their progress over time. This could be a simple checklist or a more detailed tracking sheet that allows them to note instances where they successfully applied new skills and areas for improvement.

Example: A progress tracking tool might include columns for date, context, specific skills applied, and reflections on the outcome of the communication.

Real-life Application – Workplace Training Session:

Consider a workplace training session where employees engage in role-play activities, share their experiences in group discussions, and collectively set SMART goals for improving their questioning and listening skills. The training session becomes a practical and collaborative space for continuous improvement.

By actively participating in hands-on activities, reflective exercises, and developing personalized action plans, readers can solidify their understanding of effective questioning and listening. This chapter serves as a bridge between theory and practice, empowering readers to integrate these skills into their daily lives. As readers consistently engage in these activities and monitor their progress, they will embark on a journey of continuous improvement, becoming adept communicators who contribute positively to their personal and professional environments.

Appendix:
Worksheets and Tools for
Self-Assessment

The appendix serves as a practical resource hub of exercises covered in this book under various chapters, offering readers a collection of worksheets and tools designed for self-assessment. These materials aim to facilitate active engagement with the content of the book, providing a structured way for readers to evaluate and enhance their questioning and listening skills. Let's explore the various worksheets and tools included in this book under various chapters and how to use them:

Self-Assessment Survey:
- ✓ Purpose: Evaluate your current questioning and listening skills across different dimensions.
- ✓ Example Question: *"On a scale of 1 to 10, how comfortable are you with asking open-ended questions in professional settings?"*
- ✓ Template: [Self-Assessment Survey Template]

Here is a detailed Template:
Self-Assessment Survey: Questioning and Listening Skills

Purpose: This survey is designed to help you evaluate your current questioning and listening skills across different dimensions. Please answer each question honestly and to the best of your ability.

On a scale of 1 to 10, how comfortable are you with asking open-ended questions in professional settings?

1 (Not comfortable at all)

2

3

4

5 (Neutral)

6

7

8

9

10 (Extremely comfortable)

How often do you actively listen to others without interrupting?

- ✓ Rarely
- ✓ Sometimes
- ✓ Often
- ✓ Always

Do you feel confident in your ability to paraphrase or summarize others' statements to confirm understanding?

- ✓ Yes, very confident
- ✓ Somewhat confident
- ✓ Not very confident
- ✓ Not confident at all

In a group setting, how likely are you to ask follow-up questions to clarify someone's point?

- ✓ Very likely
- ✓ Somewhat likely
- ✓ Not very likely
- ✓ Not likely at all

When faced with a disagreement, how comfortable are you with asking probing questions to explore different perspectives?

- ✓ Very comfortable
- ✓ Somewhat comfortable
- ✓ Not very comfortable

✓ Not comfortable at all

How often do you find yourself formulating your response while the other person is still speaking?

✓ Rarely
✓ Sometimes
✓ Often
✓ Always

When listening to someone, how frequently do you make eye contact to show your attentiveness?

✓ Rarely
✓ Sometimes
✓ Often
✓ Always

On a scale of 1 to 10, how effective do you think your listening skills are in building rapport with others?

1 (Not effective at all)

2

3

4

5 (Neutral)

6

7

8

9

10 (Extremely effective)

How often do you use reflective listening techniques, such as repeating back what someone has said in your own words?

✓ Rarely
✓ Sometimes
✓ Often
✓ Always

When someone expresses a strong emotion, how comfortable are you with showing empathy through your responses?

✓ Very comfortable
✓ Somewhat comfortable
✓ Not very comfortable
✓ Not comfortable at all

(Feel free to modify or add questions based on your specific needs and goals for self-assessment.)

Communication Journal Template:
✓ Purpose: Document your daily communication experiences, noting instances of successful communication, challenges faced, and lessons learned.
✓ Example Entry: *"Today, I successfully used reflective listening during a team meeting, which helped clarify misunderstandings."*
✓ Template: [Communication Journal Template]

Here is a detailed Template:
Communication Journal Template
Purpose: The purpose of this journal is to document your daily communication experiences, noting instances of successful communication, challenges faced, and lessons learned. This journal can help you reflect on your communication habits and improve your skills over time.

Date: Time: Location/Context:
Communication Experience:
✓ Describe the communication situation or interaction you had.
✓ Successes:
✓ Note any successful aspects of the communication (e.g., effective listening, clear articulation of thoughts, empathetic responses).
✓ Challenges:

- ✓ Describe any challenges you faced during the communication (e.g., difficulty in expressing thoughts, misunderstanding, distractions).
- ✓ Lessons Learned:
- ✓ Reflect on what you learned from the communication experience (e.g., the importance of active listening, the need for clarity in communication).

Action Steps for Improvement:
- ✓ Based on your reflection, outline specific steps you can take to improve your communication skills in the future.

Example Entry:

Date: [Date]

Time: [Time]

Location/Context: Team meeting

Communication Experience: During today's team meeting, we discussed the upcoming project deadline.

Successes: I successfully used active listening to understand my team members' concerns and suggestions.

Challenges: I faced a challenge in articulating my ideas clearly, which led to some confusion.

Lessons Learned: I learned the importance of clarity in communication and the need to express my thoughts more effectively.

Action Steps for Improvement: I will work on practicing clear and concise communication in future meetings.

(Feel free to customize this template based on your specific communication needs and experiences).

Goal-Setting Worksheet:
- ✓ Purpose: Set specific, measurable, achievable, relevant, and time-bound (SMART) goals for your questioning and listening skills.
- ✓ Example Goal: *"Within the next month, I will practice paraphrasing in at least three personal conversations to enhance my listening skills."*
- ✓ Template: [Goal-Setting Worksheet Template]

Here is a detailed Template:
Goal-Setting Worksheet
Purpose: The purpose of this worksheet is to help you set specific, measurable, achievable, relevant, and time-bound (SMART) goals for your questioning and listening skills. Setting SMART goals will enable you to track your progress and improve your communication abilities effectively.

Goal Statement:
Write a clear and concise statement that describes your goal.

Specific Details:
Specify what exactly you want to achieve with this goal.

Measurable Criteria:
Define how you will measure your progress and determine if you have achieved your goal.

Achievable Steps:
List the steps you need to take to reach your goal.

Relevant Factors:
Consider why this goal is important to you and how it fits into your overall communication objectives.

Time-Bound Deadline:

Set a deadline for achieving your goal to create a sense of urgency.

Example Goal:

Goal Statement: Within the next month, I will practice paraphrasing in at least three personal conversations to enhance my listening skills.

Specific Details: I will focus on restating others' statements in my own words to demonstrate active listening.

Measurable Criteria: I will track the number of conversations in which I successfully paraphrased others' statements.

Achievable Steps:

Identify opportunities for personal conversations where paraphrasing can be practiced.

Actively listen to the speaker and paraphrase their statements during the conversation.

Reflect on the effectiveness of my paraphrasing after each conversation.

Relevant Factors: Improving my paraphrasing skills will help me become a more empathetic listener and improve my overall communication effectiveness.

Time-Bound Deadline: I will complete this goal by [Date].

Reflection:

After achieving your goal, reflect on your experience and what you have learned from working towards it.

(Feel free to modify this template to suit your specific goals and communication needs.)

Progress Tracking Tool:
- ✓ Purpose: Track your progress over time, noting instances where you successfully applied new skills and areas for improvement.

- ✓ Example Entry: Date: 03/15/2024, Context: Team Meeting, Skills Applied: Active Listening, Reflection: Successfully paraphrased a colleague's suggestion for better understanding.
- ✓ Template: [Progress Tracking Tool Template]

Here is a detailed Template:
Progress Tracking Tool
Purpose: The purpose of this tool is to track your progress over time in applying new communication skills, specifically focusing on questioning and listening skills. By documenting instances where you successfully apply these skills and areas for improvement, you can enhance your communication effectiveness.

- ✓ Date: Context: Skills Applied: Reflection:
- ✓ Example Entry:
- ✓ Date: 03/15/2024
- ✓ Context: Team Meeting
- ✓ Skills Applied: Active Listening
- ✓ Reflection: Successfully paraphrased a colleague's suggestion for better understanding. This helped clarify the suggestion and encouraged further discussion within the team.
- ✓ Instructions for Use:
- ✓ Record the Date: Note the date of the communication interaction you want to track.
- ✓ Describe the Context: Briefly describe the situation or setting in which the communication took place.
- ✓ Identify the Skills Applied: Specify which communication skills (e.g., active listening,

paraphrasing, asking open-ended questions) you applied during the interaction.
- ✓ Reflect on the Outcome: Reflect on the impact of applying these skills. Note any successes, challenges faced, and lessons learned.
- ✓ Progress Summary: Summarize your progress over time, highlighting key improvements and areas for further development.

(Feel free to adapt this template to suit your specific communication goals and needs.)

360-Degree Feedback Template:
- ✓ Purpose: Collect feedback from colleagues, friends, or mentors regarding your communication style.
- ✓ Example Question: *"How would you rate my ability to ask insightful questions during our team discussions?"*
- ✓ Template: [360-Degree Feedback Template]

Here is a detailed Template:
360-Degree Feedback Template
Purpose: The purpose of this feedback questionnaire is to collect feedback from colleagues, friends, or mentors regarding your communication style. This feedback will help you gain insights into how others perceive your communication skills and areas for improvement.
Instructions: Please provide honest and constructive feedback for the following questions. Your input is valuable in helping [Name] improve their communication skills.
How would you rate [Name]'s ability to ask insightful questions during team discussions?

- ✓ Excellent
- ✓ Good
- ✓ Average
- ✓ Below Average
- ✓ Poor

In your opinion, how effectively does [Name] listen to others' perspectives during group conversations?

- ✓ Very effectively
- ✓ Effectively
- ✓ Neutral
- ✓ Ineffectively
- ✓ Very ineffectively

Does [Name] demonstrate empathy in their communication with others? Please provide examples if possible.

- ✓ Yes, consistently
- ✓ Yes, occasionally
- ✓ No, rarely
- ✓ No, never

How would you describe [Name]'s ability to communicate complex ideas clearly and concisely?

- ✓ Excellent
- ✓ Good
- ✓ Average
- ✓ Below Average
- ✓ Poor

Do you feel that [Name] effectively uses nonverbal communication (e.g., body language, facial expressions) to enhance their message? Please explain.

- ✓ Yes, always
- ✓ Yes, often
- ✓ No, rarely
- ✓ No, never

In your opinion, how well does [Name] adapt their communication style to different audiences and situations?

- ✓ Very well
- ✓ Well
- ✓ Neutral
- ✓ Poorly
- ✓ Very poorly

Overall, how would you rate [Name]'s communication skills?

- ✓ Excellent
- ✓ Good
- ✓ Average
- ✓ Below Average
- ✓ Poor

Additional Comments: Please provide any additional comments or suggestions for improving [Name]'s communication skills.

Confidentiality: Your responses will remain anonymous and will only be used for the purpose of providing feedback to [Name]. Thank you for your participation.

(Feel free to customize this template to fit your specific communication goals and the feedback you are seeking.)

How to Use the Worksheets:

Self-Assessment Survey:

- ✓ Complete the survey honestly, providing ratings and responses that reflect your current communication skills.
- ✓ Use the survey results as a baseline for identifying areas of strength and opportunities for improvement.

Communication Journal Template:
- ✓ Regularly record your communication experiences, reflecting on your successes and challenges.
- ✓ Review your journal periodically to identify patterns and areas that require focused attention.

Goal-Setting Worksheet:
- ✓ Set SMART goals based on the insights gained from the self-assessment survey and communication journal.
- ✓ Break down larger goals into manageable steps for continuous improvement.

Progress Tracking Tool:
- ✓ Use this tool to record specific instances where you applied new skills and observed progress.
- ✓ Include reflections on the outcomes of your communication efforts.

360-Degree Feedback Template:
- ✓ Seek feedback from a diverse range of individuals to gain a comprehensive understanding of your communication style.
- ✓ Use the feedback to pinpoint areas for growth and refinement.

The worksheets and tools provided throughout the book are meant to be practical companions, facilitating a hands-on approach to mastering effective questioning and listening skills. Regularly revisit these resources, update your progress, and adapt your goals as you continue on your journey of communication improvement.

May these tools serve as valuable aids in your pursuit of becoming a skilled and empathetic communicator.

Happy assessing and growing!

Conclusion: Mastering the Art of Questioning & Listening Skills

As we reach the conclusion of this insightful journey into effective questioning and listening skills, it's essential to reflect on the key takeaways and encourage the ongoing practice and application of the skills learned. Throughout this book, we've explored the intricacies of communication, delving into the art of asking the right questions and actively listening to others. Now, let's distill these insights into actionable steps for continued growth and mastery.

Summarizing Key Takeaways:

1. **The Power of Questions:** Questions are not merely tools for acquiring information; they are catalysts for deeper understanding, problem-solving, and relationship-building. By mastering the art of asking questions, you empower yourself to navigate diverse scenarios with finesse.

2. **Listening as an Act of Empathy:** Listening transcends the passive act of hearing. It's a dynamic process that involves empathy, understanding, and connection. The ability to listen actively lays the foundation for meaningful relationships, both personally and professionally.

3. **Tailoring Communication to Goals:** Effective questioning and listening are not one-size-fits-all. Tailoring your communication approach to specific goals, contexts, and individuals enhances the impact of your interactions.

4. **Continuous Improvement through Reflection:** The journey to becoming a proficient communicator is ongoing. Reflective practices, self-assessment, and goal-setting serve as compasses, guiding you toward continuous improvement in your questioning and listening skills.

Encouraging Ongoing Practice:

✓ **Create a Communication Journal:** Establish a communication journal where you document instances of successful communication, challenges faced, and lessons learned. Regularly reviewing and reflecting on these entries reinforces your commitment to ongoing improvement.

Example: After a challenging conversation, journaling about the experience can provide insights into areas for improvement and strategies to enhance your communication approach in similar situations.

✓ **Engage in Regular Feedback Sessions:** Seek feedback from trusted colleagues, friends, or mentors regarding your communication style. Constructive feedback offers valuable perspectives and helps identify blind spots that might hinder effective communication.

Example: Requesting feedback on how you handled a team meeting or a personal conversation can lead to actionable insights for refining your communication skills.

Application of Learned Skills:

✓ **Set Personal Communication Goals:** Based on the key takeaways, set specific communication goals for yourself. These goals could revolve around asking more open-ended questions, practicing active listening in specific scenarios, or enhancing your ability to tailor communication to different contexts.

Example: A personal communication goal might be to incorporate more probing questions in client meetings to deepen understanding and foster stronger relationships.

✓ **Incorporate Skills into Professional Development:** Integrate your enhanced questioning and listening skills into your professional development plan. Consider how these skills can contribute to your leadership journey, team collaboration, or client relationships.

Example: If you're a manager, incorporating active listening into your leadership style can create a more inclusive and innovative team culture.

Real-life Application – Team Workshop:
Imagine conducting a team workshop where you share the key takeaways from this book, engage in role-play activities, and collaboratively set communication goals. By fostering a culture of continuous improvement, the team collectively embraces and applies the learned skills in their day-to-day interactions.

A Lifelong Journey of Communication Mastery:
In concluding this exploration into effective questioning and listening skills, remember that communication mastery is a lifelong journey. It's not about achieving perfection but about consistently striving for improvement. As you navigate diverse communication landscapes, approach each

interaction with intentionality, curiosity, and the genuine desire to connect with others.

Continue to refine your skills, adapt to new challenges, and embrace the evolving nature of communication. By embodying the principles discussed in this book and integrating them into your daily interactions, you pave the way for richer relationships, more effective collaboration, and a profound impact on those around you.
May your journey of mastering the art of questioning and listening be both fulfilling and transformative.

Happy communicating!

About the Author
'GERARD ASSEY'

Gerard Assey is a Graduate in Economics, a PGD in Management (HRD) and holds a Doctorate in Leadership. Gerard holds several International Qualifications in Sales, Debt Collection, Training & Teaching, and is a 'Fellow' of the prestigious 'Institute of Sales & Marketing Management'-UK, a Certified NLP Practitioner, a 'Certified Trainer', an 'Accredited Management Teacher-Behavioral Sciences', a 'Certified Competency Facilitator', a 'Certified Management Consultant'- (the International credentials of a professional management consultant, awarded in accordance with global standards of the ICMCI); and a Certification from the University of Michigan in 'Successful Negotiation: Essential Strategies and Skills'

He is also a Member of the 'National Association of Sales Professionals' backed with several years experience in varied industries, both in India and Overseas. He also holds an 'Etiquette Consultant' Certification from the USA (by Sue Fox, Author of Best Seller: 'Business Etiquette for Dummies'. She has trained some of the top celebrities' world over). He was also a recipient of a scholarship for extensive training in Japan on 'Corporate Management for India'.

Gerard Assey is 'Founder & Chief Corporate Trainer' of the Group: **'Citius, Altius, Fortius Unlimited'**- an organization that **celebrated 20 years of Glorious Service** in 2021, focusing on 3 Core Competencies:

People. Performance. Profit; in functional areas of Sales & Marketing, HR & Organizational Development, covering Recruitment, Training & Consultancy!

Having managed organizations with large Sales Forces in India & Overseas, his specialization cover extensive areas of Sales Training (All levels - Presentation, Negotiation, Key/ Strategic Accounts Management & Managerial Skills for all sectors), Bid Proposal/ Capture Planning/ Management Trainings, Retail Sales, Customer Service & Customer Retention Programs, Training for Prevention & Collection of Debt, Self & Personal Development Programs (Time Management, Teamwork & Team Building, Business Etiquette & Personal Grooming, Leadership & Managerial Skills, People Management Skills, Train-the-Trainer etc), including preparation of Custom-designed Business Manuals for Internal (HR, Induction, and Sales etc) & External use (Instruction, User Manuals).

Gerard has successfully conducted over 6080 Trainings & Workshops (as of Feb '24) all across India, Middle East, Africa, Europe & S.E. Asia. Besides public programs conducted regularly, both in India & Overseas, he has some of the top names as clients whom he services from Single Owners to large Public & Government undertakings, covering all sectors, for their in-house needs.

His website: www.CollectionSkills.com is the only one in this part of the world to be featured in the 'Collections & Credit Risk Magazine-USA' under 'Who's Who in Training' and ranks TOP, along with other websites listed below on most search engines.

Gerard is author of 112 books already (Feb 2024)

A few of our business related books:

1. Bite-sized Bits on Commonsense Management
2. Heart to Heart on Life's Principles'
3. How to become a Successful Manager
4. The Sales Professionals' Master Workbook of S.Y.S.T.E.M.S
5. The Professional Business Email Etiquette Handbook & Guide
6. The Professional Business Video-Conferencing Etiquette Handbook & Guide
7. Professional Presentation Skills
8. Exceptional Customer Service
9. Professional Tele-Marketing Skills
10. Professional Debt Collection Skills
11. The G.R.E.A.T. Sales & Service Workbook
12. Sales Training Advantage for Results (*The Ultimate Sales Training Manual to enable you stand out as a S.T.A.R.*)
13. CEO Daily Planner & Organizer
14. The Sales Professionals' Master Daily Planner
15. The Professional Debt Collector's Master Daily Planner
16. My Daily Planner & Organizer
17. MY EMERGENCY INFORMATION RECORD (Family Emergency & Peace of Mind Planner)
18. The Ultimate Therapist & Counselors Planner and Organizer
19. Building an Ethical Workplace
20. Managing Relationships at Work
21. Managing Business Meetings Effectively
22. Effective Delegation Skills
23. Goal Setting for Success
24. B2B Selling by Email
25. Professional Business Etiquette & Grooming
26. Dining Etiquette & Table Manners
27. Effective Networking Skills
28. Grooming, Etiquette & Manners for Teens, Young Adults & Future Leaders
29. Inter-Personal Skills
30. Get Ready, Get Hired!
31. Selling in a Recession
32. Effective Receivables Management in an Economic Downturn!
33. Real Estate & Property Sales Training

34. Credit Sales & Accounts Receivable Management
35. Selling Skills for Real Estate & Property Advisors
36. Take G.R.E.A.T. C.A.R.E!
37. Spa, Salon & Health Club Selling Skills
38. Selling Travel, Holiday & MICE Services
39. Selling Skills for Spa's, Salons & Health Clubs
40. Retailing in Salons & Spas
41. Selling Holiday, Vacation, Tours & Packages
42. The Power of Sales Referrals
43. Selling Luxury
44. Technical Selling Skills
45. Financial Advisors Sales Training
46. Dealing with Burnout at Work Monopolize Your Markets
47. Selling to Affluent Customers
48. Growing up with Grace
49. Financial Selling Skills
50. *The Effective Manager's Guide: Key Skills to Thrive*
51. From Aspiring to Inspiring: A Guide for New Managers on the Rise
52. The Power of Focus
53. Selling with Integrity: Sell Like Jesus The Perfect Role Model!
54. 31 Habits of Champions: Your 31-Day Journey to Greatness
55. Rejecting Grasshopper Talk: From Grasshopper to Giant-Killer-*Defeating Giants Daily!*
56. Navigate the AI-Powered Future of Bid & Proposals: Up-Skill to Stay Relevant with Alternative Career Paths & Opportunities
57. Hiring Sales Winners
58. Present with Impact
59. Success Unlocked: *Breaking Free from Habits that Hold You Back*
60. Complaints to Cheers, Feedback to Gold: Mastering Complaints Management
61. Thriving Together: *Cultivating Diversity, Equity, and Inclusion*
62. Coaching Skills for Sales Managers
63. Soaring to Success in Business & Leadership: Swifter, Higher, Stronger!
64. From Classroom to Podium: A Student's Guide to Powerful Public Speaking & Presentation Skills

65. Developing Self-Discipline
66. The CEO's 31-Day Power Plan: Unlocking Success through Essential Traits
67. Credibility Matters
68. A Winning Attitude
69. Bid & Proposal Management Using AI
70. Sales Forecasting: A Practical & Proven Guide to Strategic Sales Forecasting
71. Elevate & Energize: *50 Dynamic & Fun Activities for Peak Workplace Morale*
72. 'Sales SOS! Sales on Fire! *30 Days to Conquer Chaos & the Nightmares of Success!*'
73. Mastering Sales Managerial Skills: *Building High-Performing Teams & Driving Exceptional Results*
74. Eagle-Eyed Leadership: Unleashing the Power of 31 Lessons from Eagles
75. The Ultimate Employee Training Guide: *Training Today, Leading Tomorrow*
76. Being More Accountable at Work
77. Creating a Culture of Continuous Improvement
78. Effective Questioning & Listening Skills

Besides regularly contributing to business & trade journals, including international ones such as the 'Creative Training Techniques' and the 'Sales News' of the U.S.A, He is also a member of several prestigious bodies & trade associations, having participated in many Conferences & Workshops in India & Overseas.

Prior to his last assignment of leading & managing a large MNC as head, Gerard had a 3-year stint in the Middle East as a Consultant with a leading British Consultancy Firm.

As the past 'Official Country Representative' for the International Business Award- 'THE STEVIES'-(the business world's own Oscar) for about 4 years- he ensured a few Indian companies that qualify for the same every year!

Gerard can be contacted at:
Email: training@Sales-Training.in,training@CollectionSkills.com
Websites:

       www.Sales-Training.in
       www.EtiquetteWorks.in
       www.CollectionSkills.com
       www.RetailSalesTraining.in
       www.SalesTrainingIndia.com
       www.ManualPreparation.com
       www.TrainingWithPuppets.com
       www.FirstContactAcademy.com
       www.SalesAndMarketingRecruiter.com

Our TRAININGS that can help your team

- ✓ **Sales Effectiveness**: Selling Skills for any Sector: Service/ Logistics/ FMCG Realty/ Insurance & Finance/ Media/ SPA's, Health Clubs & Salons/ Key Account Management, Effective Negotiation Skills/ Bid & Proposal Management Skills/ Retail Sales Training: Any Sector (Auto, Jewelry, Clothing, Luxury etc)
- ✓ **Customer Service Skills**-Complaints Handling & Customer Retention
- ✓ **Debt Prevention & Collection Skills**
- ✓ **Etiquette & Grooming**
- ✓ **Leadership & Managerial Skills**
- ✓ **Self & Personal Development Skills**: Presentation Skills/ Effective Communication Skills/Business Proposal Writing Skills/ Problem Solving & Decision Making Skills/ Empowering Secretaries-The perfect PA! (For Secretaries & PA's)/ Effective Time Management/ Teamwork & Teambuilding/ P.R.I.D.E- **P**ersonal **R**esponsibility **I**n **D**elivering **E**xcellence

www.ingramcontent.com/pod-product-compliance
Lightning Source LLC
Chambersburg PA
CBHW071205130726
47998CB00002B/625